HOW GOOD ARE YOU WILLING TO LET IT GET?

Daily FEELGOOD Inspiration for Creatives, Healers, and Helpers

SARAH BAMFORD SEIDELMANN

ISBN: 9780986069208

FIRST EDITION

www.followyourfeelgood.com

For Alice, and to the great power that makes everything possible.

ADVANCED PRAISE

"Once I got to ride on the back of a bull elephant. Before that experience I never realized how different the forest appears from the animal's great height, or how silently they can move. Sarah Seidelmann's book How Good Are You Willing to Let It Get? took me right back to this experience. Seidelmann's transcribed instructions from Alice the Elephant bring a sense of higher meaning, softness, humor, and beauty to our human voyage through a difficult world (and the cards bearing her art are worth at least a thousand words apiece). Sarah Seidelmann is a true medicine woman, and everything she creates is good for what ails us."

—Martha Beck, New York Times best selling author of *Expecting Adam* and *Finding Your Way in a Wild New World*

"I love Alice. In fact, I NEED Alice. So I am eternally grateful to Sarah for putting Alice's salty, nourishing wisdom into human language so we can all read it! For all you tender fierce hearts out there-- here is the daily spiritual vitamin you've been longing for."

—Katherine North, author of *Holy Heathen: A Spiritual Memoir*

" How Good Are You Willing to Let it Get is guaranteed to lift your mood, put a spring in your step, and pull you out of whatever funk that old logical brain of yours has plunged you into at any given moment. We all need help keeping our vibration high so that life gets better and better. And we all need validation for when things aren't so great. This book and card deck are designed to assist with this level of human homework. Enjoy them."

—Christiane Northrup, M.D., New York Times best-selling author of *Goddesses Never Age, The Wisdom of Menopause,* and *Women's Bodies, Women's Wisdom*

"Sarah has done it again! These daily inspirations will leave you feeling supported, inspired, and uplifted for your day, topped off with a dose of laughter. Just what the shaman ordered!"

—Tisha Morris, author of *Clutter Intervention*

OTHER BOOKS AND THINGS
BY SARAH BAMFORD SEIDELMANN

Swimming with Elephants: My Unexpected Pilgrimage from Physician to Healer

The Book of Beasties: Your A-Z Guide to the Illuminating Wisdom of Spirit Animals

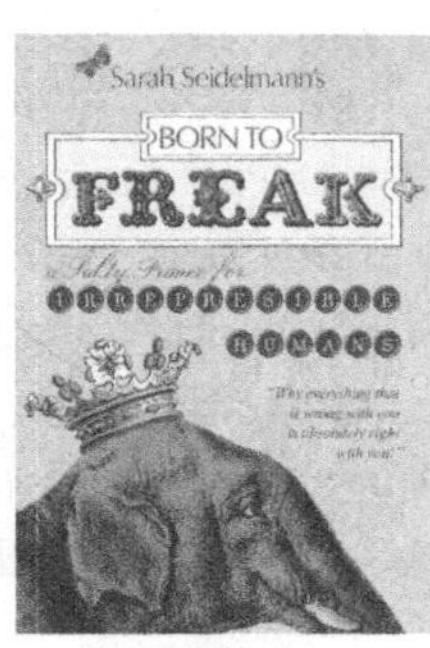

Born to FREAK: A Salty Primer for Irepressible Humans

What the Walrus Knows
app for
iPad and iPhone

How Good Are You Willing to Let it Get?
Card Deck

Available at
www.FollowYourFeelGood.com

Commit to believing you deserve to experience all the love and connection your heart desires. No earning or repenting or serving time is required. (Elephants never forget this.)
~*Born to FREAK,*
the bookie
borntoFREAK.com

INTRODUCTION by Sarah

Greetings dear creators of wonder and magic,

When I was in my early forties, I entered a midlife crisis as a physician and came out the other side as a shamanic healer, a life coach (or as I prefer to refer to myself, a Life Obstacle Assassin), and a creative / writer. I decided to dedicate my life to doing work that creates health in myself and others. I've discovered a very special subset of people (that's us!) who are healers, artists, and helpers. We have magical powers, and we have unique challenges too. I wrote this book for all of us.

Bringing newness out of the dark and mysterious cosmic womb of creation can be a delicious process, but for most of us starting out it's flabbergastingly daunting. I speak from experience. My full-throttle creative life began when I made room for it. Soon after that a helper appeared. Her name is Alice the Elephant. I highly recommend you seek out a helper in the spirit world yourself. Without Alice's superlative counsel and love, I'd still be scared, faithless, and frozen in place, afraid to make a move. Alice's advice hasn't always been easy to swallow, but it's served me so well I thought you might like it too.

As I began to visit Alice every day, asking her to share a message with me that could be shared publicly, a marvelous thing happened. People liked it! I made simple art pieces to go with Alice's missives, using words and public-domain art. The comments keep coming. "I love this!" "Yes, more Alice!" "Thank you, Alice!" It was helping people, which was fun.

One weekend, I stopped posting, because I was busy with a retreat. On Saturday, somebody messaged me, saying, "Where did Alice go? I was counting on her today!" I realized this was important work. People needed Alice. I felt excited, because feeling useful is the best feeling in the world.

I decided I'd take that little idea and hatch it into a book of daily inspirations, one for every day of the year. After each day's Alice lesson, I'd add my own commentary, an invitation or suggestion, and finally a prayer. I phoned up Grace Kerina, my dear friend and editor, and she thought the idea was smashing too.

As I reread the finished book, I see many themes: prayer, meditation, humility, moderation, self-love, family, friendship, creativity, pitfalls and quagmires, recovery from addiction, and dealing with fear. I had so much fun reviewing old lessons and learning new ones from Alice.

There is much the spirit animals can teach us. If you don't have a connection to yours yet, I highly suggest seeking one out. If you go to www.followyourfeelgood.com and subscribe, you'll get taken directly to a recording where I will guide you to connect with your spirit animal.

I send you lots of love and a freight train fully-loaded with courage and willingness.

Duluth, Minnesota

INTRODUCTION by Alice

Hello sweet beloveds! I was so chuffed when Sarah told me she wanted more of my wisdom so she could offer it to you. It's so wonderful to be honored in the world you all share. I have so many lessons to deliver to you! And I am not alone. At times, I will speak on behalf of all of the helping spirits in both human and animal form.

Your time here on Earth is more precious than you may realize, and many humans remain distracted until it's too late. But that won't be you! Let's get a move on, shall we?

ÉCHALE GANAS!
Have the courage to do your thing!

Alice the Elephant

P.S. If you forget everything else you read in this book, remember this: **RELAX.** This will keep you out of a lot of trouble.

CONTENTS

CONTENTS

January

JANUARY 1

KNIT PEACE

ALICE THE ELEPHANT

"If you want to be useful to this world, begin the day with knitting peace in your heart by spending quiet time with your Creator. Meditate. Pray. Over time, you'll create an afghan of calm to wrap around yourself and others who need it. This is the pinnacle of being useful. Through extended devotion, these serene masterpieces of the heart can bring holy coziness to a mob."

SARAH

I HAD LOTS OF "BAG LADY" fears when I left my medical practice and began working with Alice and other spirits. I asked my spirits how to find financial freedom. Their response was to teach me how to meditate. I tried it for a few days, but quickly lost interest. I returned to my spirits a month later with the same question. Patiently, they repeated their instruction. Suddenly, I felt embarrassed. I hadn't honored their message. I became willing to sit more regularly. Thousands of meditations later, I see why they made their recommendation. I've found freedom there.

Are you willing to meditate today?
When and how?

Dear God, please knit peace in my heart so I may be free.

JANUARY 2

KEEP PEDALING

ALICE THE ELEPHANT

"As you hurtle toward your highest destiny, there will be trouble along the way. Naysayers, traffic jams, and times when you fall off the bike altogether. Climb back on, remember to ring that mother f%#ing bell on your handlebars, and keep pedaling! Invisible forces will buoy you."

SARAH

I'VE DISCOVERED THAT EVERYTHING WORTH doing will include troublesome bits. For example, I'll wonder whether spending more resources on a creative project is "a beautiful act of faith" or just delusional thinking. Or the spirit-guided novel I worked on for 18 months (and that meant so much to me!) is shot down by a literary agent in New York City who I've never met (and who I'm pretty sure I would not want to invite to dinner). When you're struggling creatively, take a pause and get some rest. Phone a kind friend. Try to remember why you wanted so much to make this happen. I bet it was for a damn good reason.

Whenever things get tough, remember why your heart wants what it wants.

Dear God, help me remember what matters most so I can navigate my creative path with grace.

YOU BELONG

ALICE THE ELEPHANT

"Tend lovingly to your friendships and be open to new ones. Connect and get together often. You feed each other when you share experiences. When you're in good company, life can be exquisite. You belong to each other."

SARAH

I USED TO IMAGINE THAT "EVERYBODY else" had really good friends, or that "everybody else" was having way more fun than I was, because something was wrong with me. Horribly, that felt true recently, even when I had many amazing and dear friends around me! This is the dubious perception some of us periodically suffer. Once I become convinced of my absolute friendlessness, I can have a strong tendency to isolate myself. The best antidote is to invite a friend (old or new) for a walk or for lunch. This can feel vulnerable. What if they don't want to go? What if I'm no fun to be around? Not infrequently, some wonderful soul will say yes!

Who could you connect with today?

Dear God, help me tend my friendships and be willing to instigate new connections so we all experience more love and belonging.

JANUARY 4

REVEAL YOUR GLORY

ALICE THE ELEPHANT

"Can I tell you a secret? You are the only one who knows the singularity inside you. It's your sacred assignment to express this you-ness in everything you do. Don't deny us! Reveal your glory. This is creation."

SARAH

THE MYRIAD OF MY PREFERENCES that make me who I am include: primary colors, decoupage, old-timey images, shamanic traditions, pugs, tribal textiles, and a certain style of salty and silly irreverence. Sure, a lot of people like pugs, but not all who enjoy pugs possess the same precise patchwork of interests that I do. My tastes have been the most obvious ways for me to know I'm one of a kind. You have your own peculiar salad of things you adore. Have you catalogued them?

Find a way today to express some of your you-ness by bringing something of your glorious gumbo to the forefront. If you've forgotten what delights you, devote some time today to being curious.

Dear God, help me remember what makes me unique so I may use this specialness to serve and delight the greater good.

HAND TO HEART

ALICE THE ELEPHANT

"When you're hand-wringing over a loved one, panicked about the state of the union, or desperately wishing someone else would (for fuck's sake already!) change their horrible ways, do this: put your hand on your heart, take a deep breath, and smile. Be grateful and be here."

SARAH

OH, THE FRETTINGS I'VE HAD in this lifetime about gun violence, my children, and the spiritual guru who may (or may not?) have a dark side. I can get so caught up in thinking about the past (I should have taken the kids to church! They'll probably all join a cult!), the future (What if that yoga guy is bad?!). I have to calmly remind myself that all of this is God's business. Putting my hand on my heart always reminds me of the powerful and mysterious force that, for the moment, beats my heart and that put me here. I calm down. I return to minding my own beeswax. And there is plenty to do here now.

Place your hand over your heart and thank it for its labor.

Dear God, help me stay in my lane.

JANUARY 6

OPEN

ALICE THE ELEPHANT

"If you want to feel good, open all your receiving channels: put your feet in the river, sink your teeth into ripe fruit, allow breezes to tickle your cheek, listen to the music. Allow the force of creation to flow through you."

SARAH

I ONCE SPENT AN HOUR IN the presence of Ram Dass, who was an American spiritual teacher to many. He was rolled before us in a wheelchair. He looked lovingly out at us. After a solid ten minutes of silence, he began, very quietly, to repeat one phrase again and again: "I am loving awareness." We all soon joined him. It was a profound moment. Something opened in me. Isn't loving awareness all we've ever wanted to be? (Well, unless you're like me, and you also wanted to be Mother of the Year and be approved of by absolutely everyone). Ram Dass said that this mantra—"I am loving awareness"—was the fastest route he knew to travel from the head to the heart.

Try saying the mantra "I am loving awareness" to yourself twelve times.

Dear God, may your loving awareness pulse through me so I can do great work today.

BE CURIOUS

ALICE THE ELEPHANT

"Beauty is a medicine! Do not judge its form: voluptuous suntanned bosom, faded peony blossom, toothless grin, or fallen 300-year-old sequoia in the woods. Be curious about the mystery behind this refinement."

SARAH

As a child, I was drawn to artists like Monet and Renoir, with their flowers and gardens filled with obvious beauty. But as I've grown older, I've come to see how many artists find beauty in what society and culture deem ugly, decayed, or past its due date. For example, John Derian, my decoupage hero, keeps vases of peonies around until the blossoms are utterly devitalized. Something tender and pure emerges in their post-blossoming collapse.

Be curious and seek out beauty everywhere today—in the decay, and in the non-Instagram-y scenes all around you.

Dear God, help me see loveliness in everyone and everything so I might walk in beauty every day.

JANUARY 8

RETURN HOME

ALICE THE ELEPHANT

"Whenever you're flummoxed, go to ground. Lie down, preferably on the earth. Go boneless to get home. From this place, you'll know what should happen next, which is often nothing."

SARAH

YEARS AGO, WHEN I WAS on a "radical sabbatical" from medical practice, I had the opportunity to fall back in love with the same forest that had been the territory of my childhood. It wowed me how therapeutic a walk in those woods could be, no matter how curmudgeonly I felt. I learned that nature possesses potent healing and harmonizing qualities. During that dramatic period, I often felt tuckered out. One day, in a state, I threw myself onto the earth (much like Alice is suggesting) and, I swear, like I was a cell phone lying in a charging cradle, I felt the earth empower me and soothe my jangled nerves. I was home.

What place in nature recharges you?

Dear God, help me remember I can rest my weary carcass and recharge in your infinite largesse.

TASTE IT

ALICE THE ELEPHANT

"When Tiger hunts, every hair, each muscle, and all beats of her heart focus on one thing: the object of her desire. Even before she finds it, she tastes it. She trusts. To foster your dreams, set down that ridiculous phone, shake loose your distractions, and become Tiger."

SARAH

THE SACRED JAPANESE ART OF Kyūdō, a form of archery, is considered by many to be the purest form of martial art. One of the principles of Kyūdō that excites me is that if you want your arrow to strike the target, you must become the target. In other words, if I believe that a certain goal will bring me peace and calm, then to achieve that goal I must embody peace and calm.

What feelings do you believe your biggest dream will bring you? How could you embody that state today?

Dear God, help me hone a Tiger-like focus.

JANUARY 10

GROW YOUR HEART

ALICE THE ELEPHANT

"I double-dog-dare you to love a little something about everyone. Yeah, even that guy! Especially that guy. He (and everyone else) possesses at least one redeeming quality. Find it. Be creative. Remember, in spirit, you are all one: he is you and you are him. This is how you grow your heart."

SARAH

When I catch myself thinking frosty thoughts about someone, I step back and begin to look for the good. If I want peace, I must avoid resentment like a mofo. A beloved shaman and teacher of mine once shared this (I paraphrase): "You can pray for a whole lifetime for yourself and nothing might happen, but, if you pray for one other person, something might change. As you pray for their peace and happiness, even without telling them you are doing so, at some point they will have a knowing that it was you who prayed for them. And then, magically, when you most need the help, they will automatically begin praying for you." Reciprocity is how spirit works.

What would your prayer be for that person you feel frosty toward?

Dear God, help me pray today for a person I'm resenting. May they be happy.

ART HEALS

ALICE THE ELEPHANT

"Art heals. Make it. Wear it. View it. Listen to it. Touch it. It is a form of medicine."

SARAH

MY FRIEND PETER CREATES AMAZING mobiles of different shapes and sizes. After a consultation, he transformed our plain living room ceiling into a field of dancing pink and coral peony blooms that spiral, twist, and turn. Peony plants are a powerful symbol for me of the largesse of the Great Spirit, because of the spectacular blooms they produce with so little effort on my part. Every morning when I sit beneath Peter's art and meditate, I'm grateful. I feel stronger and more vital when I wear the necklaces my friend Tamara makes, the earrings my friend Tia makes, and whenever I listen to my friend Lauren's music. Art buoys me up, connects me to Source, and makes my life infinitely better.

Say, "Thank you," in person or online, today to an artist who has made your life better.

Dear God, thank you for all the artists who have enhanced my life experience.

JANUARY 12

BE WILLING

ALICE THE ELEPHANT

"Resting in stillness weaves an unfathomable harmony into the whole. Be willing to do this important task daily and everything will get better. Promise."

SARAH

I'VE BEEN A WORKER BEE, "type A," driven sort of person for as long as I can remember. At first, sitting still in meditation made me horribly uncomfortable. I had to keep a pad of paper nearby so I could anxiously write down all the things I worried I'd forget. Over time, meditation has become easier. I no longer need a pad of paper. I trust that it's okay to be still. I trust that good things will flow from the peaceful inner silence. I'll remember what I need to when it's time. Meditation is the greatest gift I give my friends and family, because we are all connected. That blissfulness ripples out of me.

Have you practiced stillness today? If not, would you be willing to set a timer for five minutes and be still now?

Dear God, please join me in my meditation. I need your help to become still.

FORGET FINISHING

ALICE THE ELEPHANT

"Don't try to get it all done in an hour or even in one day. There will be time for everything that matters. Relax and focus on the single most important thing now. Do it with all of your presence. Everything else will become clear."

SARAH

SOME WEEKS MY TO-DO LIST is long. Or I'm not enjoying a particular project because I feel pressure to complete it. I have a tendency to want to be constantly productive. I drive myself crazy. That tendency to get everything done because then I can relax is an unhelpful head-trip. When I relax first, everything becomes eminently more doable. I've also learned that some things I just never get to, and that's okay too.

Use this mantra today: "Everything that needs to get done will be done."

Dear God, guide me into relaxation so I can be present in everything I do today.

HOW GOOD ARE YOU WILLING TO LET IT GET?

JANUARY 14

TRUST

ALICE THE ELEPHANT

"The sun rises and shines on each of us. When other beings suffer, take whatever helpful actions you're able to, from where you stand. And be damn sure to bask in those glorious rays yourself. Trust that divine radiance touches everyone, everywhere."

SARAH

I'D SCHEDULED TIME TO WORK on a writing project, but the project wasn't working. I was frustrated. To make matters worse, I began to feel guilty that I had "free time" when, all over the world, others were suffering. Gaaaah! Alice reminded me that while, yes, there is suffering, it is also true that all beings are connected to this great power—God, or whatever name you call the amazingness that is everywhere. "It's your job," she assured me, "not to suffer, but to be helpful where you can be." Suddenly, I thought of a different writing project that might help others. I sat down and began writing.

What would change if you trusted that all beings are being tended by the Great Mystery?

Dear God, show me what you want me to do and how you want me to do it. Help me be useful in this world.

JANUARY 15

SURRENDER

ALICE THE ELEPHANT

"When the prevailing winds die down and nothing seems to be happening, your brain may desperately try to get you to do something, anything, to avoid the lull. Surrender instead. Yield to the quietude. A new gust will eventually come and fill your sails again."

SARAH

THE DOLDRUMS CAN BE A really hard place for me. I fiercely love action. Usually, fantasies of kitchen remodels, getting a whole new wardrobe, or applying minimalistic principles to all three stories of the house habitually dance in my brain. The somewhat predictable lulls in creativity used to scare me (and make our VISA bill skyrocket). Now I recognize them as being a natural part (even if not my favorite part) of the creative cycle. Surrendering to the quietude, for me, looks like taking long meanders in the woods, learning fun new things, and cleaning up messes and organizing. I think of those times as getting ready. Getting limber. Getting clear. Opening up to whatever wants to happen next.

When you're in the creative doldrums, how do you respond?

Dear God, help me use windless periods wisely.

JANUARY 16

PAMPER OFTEN

ALICE THE ELEPHANT

"Yes, you've got lots of work to do. But be sure to stop and pamper often. Paint vampire burgundy on your toenails, use the pretty crystal goblet for your Kool-Aid, slather your body in holy oil. Pampering will make you nicer to be around."

SARAH

I HAVE AN INNER CRITIC I like to call "Sister Sacrifice." She's a brusque and intimidating nun with a pair of nunchuks. When I soak in the tub on a Monday morning or book a massage, her voice can get loud. She will scold, "Good people are not idle and indulgent!" My highest self has to gently remind her that it's okay and beneficial for me to treat myself with loving kindness. Offering myself delight recharges my compassion battery.

How might you be good to yourself today?

Dear God, teach me how to find a balance between tending myself and tending the world.

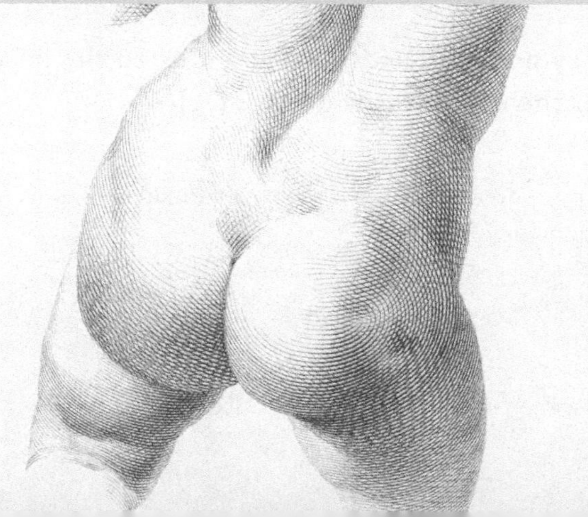

REDUCE VELOCITY

ALICE THE ELEPHANT

"Move more slowly for a minute. Super slowly. Take a look around. From this reduced velocity, a new dimension will open. You'll be able to access the languorous unfolding of a peony, the ecstatic bubbles rising in a glass of prosecco, or the kindly salutations of a wagging treetop."

SARAH

Sometimes I race from one task to another like I'm being chased by invisible hyenas. In college, I learned how this looked to others when someone did a skit ridiculing my deranged "Richard Simmons on a mission" style of race-walking across campus. It horrified me to realize people found me and my speediness so hilarious. Through the years, I've grown to love my inner racehorse. She enjoys walking fast with a dear friend at 5:30 a.m. several mornings a week. She's welcome there. I've also learned that slowing down has amazing benefits. I've discovered it's nearly impossible for me to speed-walk in the woods. The dominant, unhurried pace of the wild won't allow it.

Try going outside and attuning to the pace of the earth. How do you feel?

Dear God, help me move slowly so I may witness your amazingness.

JANUARY 18

PRAISE LIFE

ALICE THE ELEPHANT

"Find a way each day to celebrate the sacred force that flows through everything. Play the ukulele, generously compliment everyone you meet, encourage flowers to bloom, be a flash mob of one. Praise life in your own way. It's why you're here!"

SARAH

WHEN I BEGAN LONGING FOR more meaning in my life, I discovered the old-timey art of decoupage. As I glued beautiful vintage images of wild animals and flowers onto different objects I discovered a strange joy. But then I worried. Why was I doing it? I didn't want to sell the stuff I was making. Decoupage took up time and money. What was the point? It took me months to realize there was no need for the activity to have purpose, as long as it was fun. Those wild images, eventually, led to the discovery of a whole new world of animal spirits. Being creative is a form of praising life and so is play, in all of its forms.

What are some ways you could you praise life today?

Dear God, show me how I can express my wondrous and wacky divinity today.

FEED A FRIEND

ALICE THE ELEPHANT

"You need sustenance daily to survive. But by adding beauty and good company, you can thrive. Offer to feed a friend. Make love-infused orange marmalade to spread on a crusty loaf. Set your table with flowers and feast together!"

SARAH

NOTHING MAKES ME MORE EXCITED than knowing I get to share a meal with a special friend or a group of friends. One of my ideas is, "Bread for all, and roses too," from the speech given by Helen Todd on the conditions of working women in 1910. "Bread" is the basics of life, like food, shelter, and security. "Roses," for me, signify music, art, nature, creative expression, and—especially—community.

Who could you feed with love today? What might nourish them?

Dear God, may all beings have both bread and roses.

JANUARY 20

INHABIT THE SKY

ALICE THE ELEPHANT

"Your heart is a bird that longs to be free to love everything and everyone. Open its wings each morning so it can inhabit the sky!"

SARAH

I STILL SOMETIMES WAKE UP IN fear. It's usually about something I'd said I would do, but that I fear I'm not capable of doing. Or I feel separate from everyone. This is where my morning practice comes in. As soon as I read a few pages of a favorite spiritual book, relief begins to seep in. I remember that it's not "all on me," and I'm not alone. Softly, I get over myself and remember who's really in charge. My heart's wings open again. Throughout the day there may be crash landings or times when my heart fearfully tucks its wings in tight. But, morning by morning, I'm learning to set it free.

What practices help your heart soar?

Dear God, show me how to keep my heart open so I'm free to love others well.

CONNECT

ALICE THE ELEPHANT

"You are never alone. That's your ego talking. Reach out to somebody you trust for help and connection. Humble yourself."

SARAH

IT'S A WEIRD TRICK OF the ego that I can feel lonely despite the good company surrounding me. I was recently struck by an unexplained wave of existential loneliness that was difficult to shake. One night, feeling particularly abandoned, I confessed this feeling to my son George, who happened to be home from college. "Would you want to hang out?" I inquired, searching for relief. He smiled curiously. The question might have seemed strange coming from me, his mom, someone who does things with so many people all the time. "How about we watch something together?" he kindly offered. We found an exciting spy series and settled in. Being together felt good. Over a month, we got through an entire season of episodes. Because of his kindness, I suspected George had felt lonely like that too.

Humbly reach out to somebody today. It will make you both feel better.

Dear God, remind me that humility allows me to get my needs met.

JANUARY 22

BE ALL HERE

ALICE THE ELEPHANT

"Turn toward those who are suffering. Your presence is all that's needed."

SARAH

ONE MORNING BEFORE 8:00 A.M., my phone rang. It was one of our friends, calling to tell me I needed to come over immediately. Our mutual friend's husband had committed suicide. Reeling from the news, I dressed, grabbed what I needed, and drove over. In the car, I thought about how terribly unprepared and unqualified I felt to help my friend. Hell, the most significant loss I had experienced was our sweet dog Buttercup. But this? So scary and devastating. How could I help? I calmed down for a minute and asked Alice. Her answer came swiftly: "Your presence is everything." A powerful lesson landed that day as we sat with our stunned, shocked, and bereft friend: our presence alone is a powerful medicine.

Has someone been really present for you in a crisis? What did they do or not do?

Dear God, show me how to turn toward someone who suffers. Give me the words to say, if any are needed.

CULTIVATE CLOSENESS

ALICE THE ELEPHANT

"The beauty of your life depends on cultivating closeness with the Creator-God-The Universe, or whoever you pray to. Foster that alliance and ask for help each morning."

SARAH

AT A GATHERING OF PEOPLE longing to transform our relationship with food, we were charged with asking our guides-angels-higher selves for a message that would help us. Alice gave me the message above. It struck me as so obvious. If, despite endless attempts, we've been unable to solve our problem, we are going to need bigtime help. It turned out that running on self-will and ego rendered me powerless against my food problem. It wasn't until I began praying daily for help that things began to shift. The peace and freedom that followed were indescribably wonderful.

Is there is anything you long for? Try putting it in the hands of The Great Mystery today.

Dear God, I've been unable to solve this on my own. You're the boss. Please guide me.

JANUARY 24

OFFER IT

ALICE THE ELEPHANT

"When you feel anxious, imagine placing all of your cares into your hands and then offer them up to me. Let me worry about the details. Watch what happens next!"

SARAH

THE TEACHER EXTENDED HIS UPTURNED palms in front of himself, joining them to form an open bowl shape. I copied his actions. Next, he instructed me to mentally place all the things, people, situations, and issues that were burdening me into my "bowl." We sat for a few minutes in silence as we each did that. Mine filled fast with worries. Next, he said to place all my gifts and my shortcomings into the bowl. More silence passed as I thought about my flaws and good qualities. Then, together, we lifted our full bowls up to the heavens, offered it all to God, and released it. There was something so profoundly simple and beautiful about that prayer. I felt about one hundred pounds lighter that night. I fairly floated back home.

Try this prayer right now.

Dear God, take all of me—my worries, my talents, and my imperfections—and do with me what you will. I am all yours.

MEND YOUR PART

ALICE THE ELEPHANT

"You were not put on Earth to be a saint! You are here, instead, to care about those who show up in your experience. In your yoga teacher training, at the family reunion, in your book group. Love them without reservation. The scope of your work is small, but supremely necessary."

SARAH

Sometimes, after viewing the devastating news from around the world, my heart feels overwhelmed at the scale of the pain. I long to repair it all. Such events can leave me feeling powerless, as if there's nothing I could do, short of being a Mother Theresa–like figure, that could ever be enough. Meanwhile, my efforts to get dinner on the table, to fetch kids from school, and to attend to my beloved clients don't feel sufficient. But, as Dr. Clarissa Pinkola Estés recommends, my only responsibility is to "Mend the part of the world that is within reach."

What could you mend today? What is within reach?

Dear God, remind me that my scope of work may be small, but it is not insignificant.

SEEK GUIDANCE

ALICE THE ELEPHANT

"You do not have to be 'good.' Instead, seek guidance from the silence within. There will be gentle instructions there—an approach, a direction, a recipe, a knowing. From this softness you'll find peaceful footing."

SARAH

I OFTEN RESORT TO BELIEVING EVERYTHING is either good or bad. It follows, of course, that I judge myself and others this way too. A good mother would not leave her children for twenty-one days to travel to India; therefore, a sort-of mother who goes to India is bad. For me, this kind of thinking is a trap and doesn't leave room for all the gray areas where everything true exists. The soul is not concerned with good and bad. It yearns for what it yearns for—for love—and if I try to conform to the rules of society, I might miss my hero's journey, or a sacred adventure to India.

Instead of trying to be good today, ask your heart, "What do you want me to know?"

Dear God, show me the path to take.

DELIVER JOY

ALICE THE ELEPHANT

"Deliver joy to whomever you visit today—a smile, a specific compliment, good news, a tiny gift. This will transform mere connection into communion."

SARAH

I RECENTLY HEARD ABOUT A MAN who lives at a local nursing home and mails twenty cheerful postcards a day to complete strangers. I've got a hunch his heart is pretty full. I've spent plenty of days asking, "What's in it for me?" But I've slowly been learning that an attitude of "What can I offer?" can turn an ordinary day into one spiked with ecstasy. It's a simple shift to make. As I offer good stuff to others, it is always me who gains the favor.

What would you like to do to deliver joy to somebody today? What sounds fun?

Dear God, remind me to go out of my house today like a lantern, shining on everybody I encounter.

LOSS BRINGS

ALICE THE ELEPHANT

"Death is only transformation. It is both a beginning and an ending. Be curious about what is born after a relationship, a way of behaving, or a loved one dies."

SARAH

WHEN MY FRIEND JESSEY DIED of suicide, I was in complete shock. As we gathered together to mourn him, we all realized we'd missed the signs and wished we had done things differently. In his absence, we filled the room with our stories of him. Despite the suffering he had endured, the teachings he left us with were so rich. My gratitude for his life deepened. Now, years later, he visits me in my dreams and ceremonies to remind me that he's still here for me and our friendship is without end. I hadn't predicted that his death would create a new sort of relationship between us. It is one I cherish.

Name something (a house, a relationship, a job...) or someone you have lost and consider what was born because of that loss.

Dear God, help me welcome what may come through death and other types of endings.

SIT WITH YOURSELF

ALICE THE ELEPHANT

"Early morning is a gift. Whether you sit in stillness, write, or pray matters not. What matters is that you are awake and being with yourself during this quiet time. Here is where your heart is open."

SARAH

I AM A TRUE MORNING LARK now, but I didn't used to leap out of bed at five a.m. I've grown to appreciate the sacred time of early quiet and now I grieve it when I miss it. Sitting in stillness for fifteen minutes every day helps calibrate my nervous system. Visiting this untroubled spaciousness daily has created, over the years, a deeper well for me to tap into when my day brings a little (or a lot) of chaos or adversity. As my heart settles into the quiet, more things seem possible and my capacity to handle life on life's terms grows a bit. If I want to fly, my morning practice is essential.

Do you have a morning practice? What might make that communion sweeter?

Dear God, help me find the willingness to sit in silence with myself each morning so I begin the day in your heart.

JANUARY 30

GO TO GROUND

ALICE THE ELEPHANT

"When you're all a-dither and it's apparent to you that things are spinning out of control, go outside and place both hands on the earth. From there, you'll know what's real and what's not."

SARAH

DURING HOT-MESS MOMENTS, I EVENTUALLY realize I need to interrupt the spiral of negative thinking. As I cross the threshold from the city into the wild, if I have any presence of mind left at all, I'll greet the forest out loud—"Hello!"—then I'll ask the spirit of the land to teach me what I need to learn. The woods are always extremely generous with their advice, doling it out in fluttering leaves, tender ground, shining wildflowers, or fields of silent snow. After three or four minutes, I'm fifty percent better. After an hour, I'm utterly new again. Simple solutions arise. I return home ready to face everything with an open heart.

Ask the wild to restore you today.

Dear God, teach me to be like the trees who have lived long on this earth, full of stillness and grace.

JANUARY 31

YOU ARE FREE

ALICE THE ELEPHANT

"Pridefulness is damaging. It takes you out of the river of life. The good news is that if you're feeling separate right now, the flow is only a step away. You're free to choose."

SARAH

WHILE COLLABORATING WITH SOMEONE, A lovely human being, I made a big boo-boo. In my head, I worked out a lot of things without communicating any of it with her. I felt justified about my decisions and expected her to agree with me. When she didn't, I panicked. How dare she question me? Then I sat for a minute and saw what I had done. I told pride we needed to do things differently. I confessed to my friend that I agreed with her and shared that I had a history of working everything out in my head but failing to communicate. Immediately, we found common ground again.

Whenever you notice pride, remember you are free to choose to step back into flow.

Dear God, remove my pridefulness and show me what work must be done to stay close to you.

February

LEAN INTO ME

ALICE THE ELEPHANT

"Lean into the weightiness of our connection. With me along, you can do things you previously thought impossible. Share your divinely supported successes with others. Tell them how you've been buoyed up."

SARAH

THERE'S A SAYING IN TWELVE-STEP recovery programs: "God did for me what I could not do for myself." I treasure that truth. If I believe life is up to me, trouble begins. It's too much for me to handle. I've tried and tried and tried again. Nothing works as well for me as surrendering it all, turning it over to God. The split second I turn whatever problem, person, situation, or fear over to Source, relief begins to flood my experience. Without that divine support, I cannot create magnificent things—a harmonious marriage, good relationships with my children and friends, successful creative projects.

What would you like to surrender to Source today?

Dear God, I give you all of myself today. Do with me what you like. Show me what to do and how to do it.

FEBRUARY 2

SET MIRACLES IN MOTION

ALICE THE ELEPHANT

"Be still and know that I am Alice. When you touch the silence within yourself, you tap into a spectacularly unlimited reservoir of perfectly amazing ideas: fresh color combinations to try, strange salad dressing recipes to whisk up, phone calls to make, caring commentary to provide, and never previously thought-of alliances to build. When you apply these insights, you'll set miracles in motion."

SARAH

DEAR MEDITATION, WHY DO I still resist you? I know firsthand that the quiet, still place inside me, that "no-thing-ness" is so powerful, but I am still imperfect at doing it. Even so, I keep coming back to it, spending more days meditating than I do running from it. I celebrate all the beauty and wonder that tumbles out from the silence, the glorious quietude that's strangely everything and nothing all at once. It is supreme peace.

What, if anything, keeps you from sitting in stillness?

Dear God, lift whatever keeps me from sitting in stillness today so I can help you make miracles possible.

TELL THE TRUTH

ALICE THE ELEPHANT

"Be honest with yourself. It is the foundation of everything. Commit lovingly to a strict no-bullshit policy. Did you say what you meant to say? Are you doing what you said you'd do? If the answer is 'no,' don't judge. Be kindly curious instead."

SARAH

BEING OUT OF INTEGRITY FEELS awful. For example, if I said I'd write today, but find myself, four hours later, with a clean house but zero writing done. Or, if I decide I'll have just one ripe peach, but I eat three. Or, if I tell my kid I'll be at school for pick-up, but they have to call me, wondering where I am. None of those events is lethal. But the pattern of not doing what I'd said I would do always succeeds in making me feel less alive. I begin to lose faith in myself and my abilities. I dishonor the things I truly cherish: my writing, my integrity, my attention to my kids who depend on me.

If you've been out of integrity with yourself, ask yourself why.

Dear God, help me walk in integrity with myself.

FEBRUARY 4

APPRECIATE

ALICE THE ELEPHANT

"Good luck—that 'holy smokes!' double rainbow advantage—is rained on you dreamers who appreciate how much patience things worth creating take, and who appreciate the important contributions of the characters who support you."

SARAH

WRITING AND PUBLISHING MY FIRST book required tremendous effort. At times, I wondered why it was so difficult. After writing and editing, my flummoxed brain got overwhelmed navigating the purchase of ISBNs and uploading the book files to the distributor's website. At the time, I didn't fully appreciate how blessed I was to be surrounded by such helpful people: phone support, editor, and designer. Without my willingness to hang in there and be patient, I might have given up. The more patient and appreciative I can be, the luckier I become.

Remind yourself today that things worth doing take time and lots of help. Which of your helpers could you appreciate today?

Dear God, help me see all the helpers today. Lift any frustrations and elevate my spirit so I can work mindfully and with kindness.

FOLLOW INNER NUDGES

ALICE THE ELEPHANT

"Your body is a jewel. For maximum health, ask me for help and guidance with your carcass care. Follow inner nudges throughout the day—to stretch, to eat particularly vibrant vittles at certain times, or to go boneless from time to time."

SARAH

I USED TO DRINK AND EAT to excess. I used to ignore my body's desire to dance, stretch, and move. I also forced my body to keep going when it was exhausted or ill. As I began to turn toward myself and my body again at midlife, I began to notice the times I did things that didn't feel honoring. With divine help and the help of a recovery community, I let go of substances and foods that were not beneficial. I became willing to rest when I needed to. My inner guidance knew what I needed all along. It took time and effort to follow its guidance.

Have you been ignoring your inner wisdom with regard to your body temple? Take time today to honor your carcass.

Dear God, make me willing to nourish and care for this body you've given me.

FEBRUARY 6

CREATE YOUR WAY

ALICE THE ELEPHANT

"Thinking too much can get you into trouble. I suggest you use your hands to transform things instead: arrange flowers in a tiny vase, braid hair, write a one-line song, overhaul a dusty cranny into an altar, swirl globs of paint into a never-before-seen galaxy. Creative acts connect you to me. Thinking does not."

SARAH

FOR ME, IT'S ESPECIALLY IMPORTANT to create in mediums that are not the ones I desperately want to be "good" at. I've been more willing to practice writing imperfectly, for example, since I taught myself to (imperfectly) play ukulele. I look forward to the moments when I can dabble with watercolors at the kitchen table, or take flowers into the woods to make a prayer mandala for a stranger to discover. These acts always leave me joyful and I become more willing to work on my writing, a practice I care deeply about.

Create something today in a medium that feels like play to you.

Dear God, show me how to be creative today.

HONOR TIME

ALICE THE ELEPHANT

"Pay careful attention to the unique opportunities provided by time itself: the phases of the moon, dawn / noon / dusk, the seasons of the year. Some periods are designed for taking serious action. Others invite you to rest. As you learn to honor the qualities of these periods, things will get easier."

SARAH

I ONCE READ THAT THE MOON is a better reflection of us than the sun, because the moon waxes and wanes just as our energies tend to. I usually feel amazing in the days around a full moon, even though I often don't sleep as deeply then. During elevated full moon periods, I feel more connected to spirit. When I feel a bit low-energy and need to rest more, it often correlates with the new moon. We are, after all, beings of the cosmos. It's no wonder we're impacted by her cycles.

What celestial cycles would you like to become more aware of?

Dear God, help me learn about the cycles of the moon and sun, and teach me to live in more harmony with them.

FEBRUARY 8

REPAIR

ALICE THE ELEPHANT

"Grace is everywhere. It's available in your next breath. When you've f#%ked up, breathe in understanding and exhale shame. Then go make things right. Say how you were wrong and begin taking action to set things right."

SARAH

DESPITE MY LONGING TO BE the best daughter, wife, mother, friend, sister, I still mess up on the regular. I get so mad at myself. "I just finished meditating five minutes ago! How did I end up here so quickly? What's wrong with me?" Sometimes an apology is enough, but sometime more is needed. A month ago, I said something insensitive to our sixteen-year-old daughter and saw her face fall. I knew I had misspoken. I quickly apologized and asked her what I could do to make it right. That made an enormous difference. Taking corrective action is a next-level apology.

Do you owe somebody an apology? How could you begin to make it up to them?

Dear God, help me see where I've caused harm to another so I can begin to make repairs.

BE IRREPRESSIBLE

ALICE THE ELEPHANT

"When you feel really good, don't restrain yourself. Shout it from the rooftops! Yes, there will always be tragedy and suffering. But only by appreciating the good will you gain the power to be truly helpful with the hard stuff."

SARAH

Martín Prechtel, indigenous shaman and author, says we're here on Earth for only two reasons: to grieve and to praise. To praise is to celebrate the beauty we see. To call it out and embody it. To get your hair done and present yourself in the best way you can. To tend your gardens so that flowers bloom. If you're not sure how to praise, study the people around you who have what you desire and emulate their behavior. Yes, there will be grief too, but when it comes, we'll be capable of expressing it because we have praised.

Who do you know who's masterful at feeling good? Which of their behaviors might you like to emulate?

Dear God, show me how to appreciate life more fully. Teach me how to make myself and my whole life more beautiful.

FEBRUARY 10

THRUST

ALICE THE ELEPHANT

"Try leading from your pelvis. It sounds funky, but this is the space that, energetically, holds all possibilities. It's the silent, fertile darkness. Connect with it. Walk around the block, allowing your pelvis to lead. Experience the difference between that and moving from your head."

SARAH

ACCORDING TO QUANTUM PHYSICS, WE'RE all a mess of particles and electrons in space. We're made of energy. Many ancient wisdom traditions refer to the energy body and describe wheels of light, which some traditions call chakras. Each chakra has its own frequency and qualities. Whenever I bring awareness to one of these energy centers—like the womb chakra (in the pelvis)—I become more acquainted with its energy. This can be fun! As my wise mother says, "Awareness is everything."

What do you notice when you take a walk around the block with your pelvis leading?

Dear God, help me be aware of my subtle body so I can tune in to my own energy signatures. Help me sing, pray, write, speak, and create from my unique frequency.

DEPLOY YOUR IMAGINATION

ALICE THE ELEPHANT

"When nothing is working and you feel unclear about everything, here's what to do: dream it up. What else might be possible? Ask for a divine insight and wait for it to gurgle up. Take an inspired action based on this new perception, even if it's illogical. Especially if it's illogical. Repeat daily. Results may exceed your original expectations in mysterious ways!"

SARAH

SYMPTOMS OF STUCKNESS INCLUDE CRANKINESS, generalized whining, headaches, backaches, gossiping, picking fights, drinking or eating too much or too little, sleeping in when you're not tired. As one of my favorite shamans says, "That tiredness you feel cannot be cured with more sleep." When I catch myself plastered to the bottom of a cosmic sewer or otherwise immobilized, spiritually speaking, I try to remember to open a window in my mind, to let in some fresh air and allow a moment of expansiveness.

Try taking a deep breath in and looking up. What possibilities might also exists that you hadn't yet considered?

Dear God, help me imagine my way forward.

FEBRUARY 12

WAIT

ALICE THE ELEPHANT

"Things will get stirred up. Chaos, when it arrives, is only an invitation. Retreat into yourself until the murk settles and clarity rises like a diamond."

SARAH

SOME CHOICES FEEL DIFFICULT AND chaotic. Should I go left or right? Stay or leave? Yes or no? I always like to remind myself that there are no bad choices—there's only feedback. Sometimes I try out a decision before committing to it, to explore how it feels. I imagine I've already agreed to teach a shamanism class in Beijing. If, as I feel all the way into it, it doesn't feel as good as I'd hoped, I can adjust my sails. Sometimes I seek the input of wise friends. With time, answers always come. Clarity never feels pressing. It feels light and peaceful.

In what area of your life do you crave clarity? How could you retreat into yourself for a bit today to feel around for it?

Dear God, show me the way to proceed. Give me inner nudges, angel numbers, auspicious blue cheese appetizers—whatever it takes to get my attention. I'm listening.

RESTORE

ALICE THE ELEPHANT

"When in doubt, get extra rest. Hit the hay early. During deep sleep, you'll draw closer to the truer reality. Sleep is restorative. A fresh confidence will emerge."

SARAH

ONE SPRING, I COMMITTED TO getting the sleep I needed every night. It made all the difference. Setting multiple alarms when it was time for me to go to bed helped me stay in integrity with this goal (although the nightly Alexa announcements drove everybody at home a little cray-cray). I also performed a simultaneous bedside book intervention to remove towering stacks of novels leading me into the temptation to read far too late into the night. I left only a tiny book of Rumi poems on my bedside table. Serious fiction reading had to happen elsewhere. Ample sleep impacts my confidence and my attitude tremendously.

Do you get sufficient sleep most nights? If not, what needs to shift?

Dear God, give me guidance on my sleep plan so I can fire confidently on all cylinders as I do your bidding.

FEBRUARY 14

DIVINE CARCASS

ALICE THE ELEPHANT

"Your body is a glorious apparatus designed to allow you to feel your way through this world. Each part of your body provides an opportunity to deepen your connection to life. Your lap is a comfort station. Your hands are for caressing. Your buns for are for shimmying! Treat your body as you would any astonishing and sacred treasure."

SARAH

LOOKING BACK, I SEE THAT I abused my body for years with too much booze, too many malted milk balls, not enough sensual pleasure, and not enough creative movement. Each year, as my body ages, my love and appreciation for it grows. One powerful practice I've learned is patterned after Abhyanga, a form of sacred self-massage from the Ayurvedic tradition. I whip up a bottle of extra virgin olive oil infused with essential oils. Lately, I'm loving rose, geranium, and cedar. After taking a shower, I spend a few minutes rubbing loving kindness into each part of my carcass as I massage the oil into my skin.

How could you enjoy or honor your body today?

Dear God, help me treasure my body in all its amazingness.

WISDOM BRINGS PEACE

ALICE THE ELEPHANT

"How can you tell the difference between the rubbish products of your overworked mind and divine guidance? The first will often feel mildly manic, unsure of itself, and sketchy as hell. The latter will always bring peace and, not infrequently, deep belly laughter."

SARAH

As ridiculous as it is, I still sometimes forget I can ask for divine guidance! We humans are sometimes referred to as "The Great Forgetters," and it's true. But my mind never forgets to think. It's always busy—scheming, weighing, measuring, and judging. Always. Much of my mind's activity is unhelpful. At times, it can even be downright alarming. When wisdom arrives (or is dropped on my lap by an encounter with a stranger or a beastie that wanders by) to banish the mental clamoring, it's always a great relief.

Where in your life do you need divine guidance right now? Have you asked for it?

Dear God, please guide me in everything I do and say.

FEBRUARY 16

YOU WILL BE LIFTED

ALICE THE ELEPHANT

"When darkness and despair have you in their clutches, I invite you to relax, let go, and collapse in a heap. That's when I can really help!"

SARAH

I HAVE A TENDENCY TO RESPOND to the unknown and things that frighten me by tensing my body. You should see me during a scary movie. It's ridiculous! I have such a hard time separating myself from the on-screen reality that I contort into the strangest positions. When the movie's climax arrives, I'll let out a scream or launch myself into my movie partner's lap. I do much the same thing when I get scared about life. My muscles tighten and I hold my breath. I'm learning to remind myself to relax and breathe. When I go boneless, I feel Spirit catch me and I realize there is nothing to be afraid of.

Try it now: go boneless. Do you sense anything different when you're utterly relaxed?

Dear God, help me completely relax, wherever I am.

LET ME LEAD YOU

ALICE THE ELEPHANT

"When thinking about whether things are fair in life, consider that it's all perfect. You may feel guilty about the relative ease of your life, but you don't know the ease others experience. If you were to attempt to 'endure' what you believe they are 'enduring,' simply to make things more 'fair,' you'd be making a grave mistake, and you might never reach your destiny. Stop trying to play God. Let me lead you. Capiche?"

SARAH

I USED TO WONDER (AND SOMETIMES still do) why my life feels so blessed when others are clearly suffering. Alice always sets me straight. Trying to understand why things are the way they are is not particularly helpful. Nor is feeling guilty about the good in my own life. I tend to perform much better when I make God the boss of me.

Do you ever feel guilty about the good things in your life? What happens when you let Source be the boss of all that?

Dear God, help me embrace the way things are, including the ease and the suffering. Thank you for being such a benevolent boss.

FEBRUARY 18

JUST LIKE YOU

ALICE THE ELEPHANT

"When you see someone acting like an extreme douche (ED), remember that, like you, they long to love and be loved. The two of you are harmonious in your deepest desires. It's good to ask yourself, What would make a person act like they're acting? I ask you: Why did you behave in a douche-y manner the last time you did?"

SARAH

WHEN RESENTMENT TOWARD SOMEONE POPS up for me—How could they!? or Really?—I try to remember that I too am eminently capable of being an ED. When I'm full of fear, hepped up on jealousy, exhausted, or simply anxious about everything, my communications can come out sideways. I try to simply do the next right thing. Usually, that is to decide not to take everything so personally.

When did you last catch yourself being an ED? Can you forgive yourself?

Dear God, thank you for the grace you shower on me every single day.

DARE

ALICE THE ELEPHANT

"Do the creative thing that scares you. If you can do it without too much attachment to the outcome, that's best. The lessons will be precious and profound."

SARAH

On some days I have so many creative ideas they confuse me. Certain ideas are persistent, though. Those ideas keep gurgling back up, as if to say, "Pick me!" Then I begin thinking that idea, though a bit scary, might be fine, as long as I am guaranteed that others will want it or need it, or that I won't lose money trying to do it or... fill in the blank with some other end result I must have. Those outcomes I "must have" tend to dominate me. But then a moment of grace arrives and I remember that creating for the sake of creating is always good, no matter how it all turns out.

What are you scared to do? How deeply attached are you to the outcome? Could you let go of outcomes and create anyway?

Dear God, show me the creative acts I need to act on. Help me release my attachment to outcomes.

FEBRUARY 20

HONOR WATER

ALICE THE ELEPHANT

"Celebrate water as you interact with it every day. Whether you're guzzling it, showering in it, or dropping water balloons on an unsuspecting loved one, give thanks. Water contains the signatures of life."

SARAH

VISITING MY FAVORITE TINY STREAMS, roaring rivers, and grand lakes always comforts me, because water is always in a state of allowing. Water seems utterly self-accepting and emboldened, whether it's streaming through a saturated marsh or roaring onto an unyielding stone cliff. Baptizing myself in the shower or, better yet, out in nature, always feels like a tiny rebirth. After all, we emerged at birth from a watery womb.

Pour yourself a glass of water and take a moment to thank the water for all its gifts. Ask it to bless your body. Chug with gratitude.

Dear God, thank you for amazing, crystal clear water. May it run clean and clear for all the generations to come.

FLOWERS ARE A MEDICINE

ALICE THE ELEPHANT

"Bring flowers into your space. A single bloom will suffice. At first, its essence will subtlety heal you with its beauty and unique properties. Second, it will teach you as it unfurls into intense fullness. Finally, you will learn about endings through its fading, falling apart, and returning to Source. Return spent blossoms to the earth. Replenish weekly. This practice will help you come into greater harmony with everything."

SARAH

One summer, flowers became my gurus. Saturated yellow buttercups showed me how to own my personal power. Violet stalks of lupine encouraged me to use my creative voice and trust it would be beneficial. Peonies, my favorite of all blossoms, taught me about patience, self-love, and abundance. Peony reminds me that I've always had (and always will have) more than enough. Each flower brings its own medicine.

What flower is your favorite? What bloom do you love most? How might their medicine be trying to help you?

Dear God, thank you for the flowers you give us. Help us understand their teachings so we may honor you as they do.

FEBRUARY 22

BREATHE EASY

ALICE THE ELEPHANT

"Love lands on those who are calm and breathing easy."

SARAH

SOMETIMES, IN A NEEDY MOMENT, unhelpful thoughts will claw at me and I become convinced I need something to change in order to feel good again. Or I'm absolutely certain my worth is directly proportional to my Amazon author ranking. Those moments are unpleasant. Remembering to relax and breathe always breaks my egoic trance and allows a distinctive sweetness to return. The dog leans in for a belly rub. Nothing more needs to happen. I only need to do the next thing in the best way I know how.

Try taking a deep breath now. Exhale, and see if you can perceive love landing.

Dear God, help me stop wishing circumstances were different so I can be here now.

GRATITUDE STRENGTHENS

ALICE THE ELEPHANT

"In time, everything and everyone on Earth dies. It is good to grieve. And it is good to find gratitude right now for the things and beings who remain. Gratitude gives you the strength to tend your life. Gratitude is an expression of love and, as such, will never die."

SARAH

WILD FIRES BURNED OUT OF control in the Amazon, destroying the lives of many innocent creatures, including the incredible trees. I felt overwhelmed. What could I do in the face of such an overwhelming tragedy? I sent a donation to help the local native people in their mission to defend the rainforest from corporate greed. Next, I went to Alice to ask what else I could do and she gave me the message above. While visiting her, I cried, not realizing I had bottled up my grief. After that visit, I began to do as she'd suggested and give thanks for all the beautiful life around me.

How could you express your grief for what's been lost as well as your gratitude for what remains?

Dear God, help me grieve and be grateful.

FEBRUARY 24

LOOSEN UP

ALICE THE ELEPHANT

"Today is a very good day to play. Loosen up. Open to new options. Laugh at your peculiar ridiculousness. Wear those flashy earrings you usually eschew. Ask a dog or cat for spiritual advice. Roll down a grassy knoll. This will allow us to send more of the good stuff through you."

SARAH

I NEVER USED TO GIVE MUCH thought to what I wore. That was before I discovered that everything that is, is alive, and has a vibration, a spirit. Now when I get dressed (especially if I'm feeling out of sorts!), I pick out mood-boosting outfits and accessories. I enjoy a pediatric fashion sensibility: electric yellow earrings made by a friend, a t-shirt with white rabbits on it. I prefer anything that feels a little looser, more magical, or more playful. Dressed this way, I feel more open to a state of wonder.

In what ways could you embrace a state of play today?

Dear God, help me relax and be playful today!

BLOOM ANYWAY

ALICE THE ELEPHANT

"Despite desperate circumstances—extreme heat, lack of water, relentless winds—the cactus blooms. To bloom under unusually challenging conditions, be present to the frequency of the here and now. Then shoot love lasers out your eyes, hug enthusiastically, and be unwavering in your service to the creative force."

SARAH

THE DESERT IS A FUNNY place. It's so different from the dense, humid boreal forest I'm more familiar with. Yet, despite the relative lack of water and the intensity of the sun, the same Great Power is present. We can align with this power too. We do it with presence. When I breathe, pay attention, and focus with open awareness on my surroundings, I bloom just as Alice suggests. No matter what.

Bring yourself to the present moment. What would it be like to share this beautiful creative force with others?

Dear God, when things get challenging, teach me to tap into your infinite presence.

FEBRUARY 26

BE ROOTED

ALICE THE ELEPHANT

"Imagine you're standing in front of an unbelievably powerful industrial fan. It's so forceful that, at any moment, you might tumble backwards. That is how difficult it can be to stay in integrity with yourself. Willpower is of little use. When forces threaten to topple your conviction, sense the inner tether connecting you to the divine. It will hold you steady."

SARAH

WHEN I REALIZED I WAS unable to keep promises to myself, I decided to work on my integrity by working on my relationship to food. I'd either eat more than I'd said I would, or I'd eat some non-nourishing food I'd committed to avoiding. There was my lack of integrity. After a lifetime of attempting to control food, I realized I was unable to do it. With the help of a spiritual program, I learned to admit I was powerless and ask God to direct me. Suddenly, I was able to stay in integrity with myself. It was a miracle.

In what ways do you struggle to stay in integrity with yourself? Are you willing to ask for direction from Source?

Dear God, lend me your power so I may do with you what I cannot do for myself alone.

EXPECT MIRACLES

ALICE THE ELEPHANT

"Petition, petition, petition! We can't do much without a request. Whether you want to feel closer to the divine, or you need a good deal on a used Toyota RAV4, asking is critical. Expect miracles. Little by little, you'll come to understand that, while not everything is meant for you, no heartfelt request goes unanswered."

SARAH

WE NEEDED A USED CAR on a tight budget and had three hours to get it. I knew, from past experience, that buying a decent used car could take a lot longer, so I prayed for a sign to show us which car to purchase. We got to the dealership and test drove the first option: not enough head room. The second car that fit our criteria had just been turned in and hadn't yet been cleaned up. My husband Mark opened the door and discovered a yard sign in the back seat from a wedding reception that said, "Mark and Sarah." We grinned at each other. Thanks to that "sign," we made the fastest used car purchase in our history. It's been a great car. I regularly pat its dashboard gently to say thanks!

Pray today for help with something that feels difficult.

Dear God, give me signs to direct me on my path.

FEBRUARY 28

SWIM IN IT

ALICE THE ELEPHANT

"Cash is a subject you tend to think an awful lot about. I recommend you stand knee-deep in the river and really feel the flow of life. The sensation of lack often emerges when you're mentally rehashing a past "financial debacle"—which, by the way, was not really a debacle, but just what happened, or you're anxiously trying to manage future fiscal events. When you feel poor, step back into the flow. Swim in it! Revel! Playfully invite someone who's stuck on shore to join you! This experience is all you've ever really longed for anyway."

SARAH

I OFTEN MARVEL AT HOW MANY gazillions of moments I've squandered wringing my hands over things that have to do with money (making it, spending it, giving it away) when, all along, I was being carried joyfully by the river of life. When anxious thoughts of lack arise, I remind myself I've always been okay and, as Alice promises, I always will be.

Who would you like to "swim" with in the abundant river of life today?

Dear God, help me trust that I always have exactly what I need.

March

MARCH 1

LOOK OUT

ALICE THE ELEPHANT

"Exposing yourself to certain types of media may have you concluding that the world is a dark and dangerous place. But if you abstain from such sources and, instead, ingest fortifying dispatches, you'll become more capable of seeing the magnificence. You'll likely find grand, friendly trees, kind people, and gentle breezes around every corner. Even during an apocalypse."

SARAH

When our oldest son was little, I noticed how fearful he got after the smallest exposure to the television news. I stopped watching network news, but worried about becoming uninformed. Instead, I discovered that I learned what I needed to know through other sources, like a friend telling me. Now I feed myself a steady diet of Sufi poetry, words from inspiring thought leaders, and what I consider to be news of holy goodness. These media sources train my brain away from looking for what is wrong with the world, and toward seeing what is right.

How could you abstain today from any media that leaves you dispirited?

Dear God, direct me to sources of media that nourish my soul.

MARCH 2

LISTEN

ALICE THE ELEPHANT

"When someone is distressed, there's a powerful and peculiar way to be of service. The solution is so simple it may be tempting to complicate it. Don't. Sense your feet on the ground, your heart nestled in your chest, and listen. Like a motherfucker. Resist the temptation to add to their story of woe or to offer your sage advice. If you can't control your urge to advise, you could ask, 'Would you like to hear my input?' But I think you'll find that even that can sometimes be a misstep."

SARAH

IT USED TO BE EXCRUCIATING for me when anybody was upset. Especially if it was one of my beloveds. When they suffered, I suffered. I wanted to fix it. I believed that if I could just say the right thing or give them proper instruction, things would improve. With Alice's tutelage, I've learned, little by little, to resist that urge and, instead, call upon the salty saint I like to call "Our Holy Father of Shut-the-Fuck-Up." He is all-powerful.

When you meet someone who's upset, try calling upon the salty saint and just listen.

Dear God, remind today me of the supreme power of shutting my mouth.

MARCH 3

KEEP GOING

ALICE THE ELEPHANT

"You have a brilliant, crystal clear idea for something. Hours or weeks later, overwhelm descends, and the beautiful sparkle dims. Suddenly, it feels too risky, not profitable, or simply impossible. First, calm down. Ideas worth doing take time, patience, and help from others. Keep exploring the idea: make a call, ask people you admire how they'd approach it, create a mood board, immerse yourself in yummy research. And remember the thrilling, sweet, boundless flourish with which the idea landed."

SARAH

We artists and healers have so many different ideas and dreams that come to us from Source. They are valuable, and I've learned to give them life: to speak them out loud, write them down, or make collages of them. The fears always follow. Am I capable? Will anybody care? Is it weird? Am I misdirected? Allowing myself to explore my ideas ensures that the very best ones will find the light of day and, with the help of others, I will see them become reality.

What exciting idea of yours has fear squashed? How might you keep exploring that idea anyway?

Dear God, please banish my fears of creating.

EMBRACE

ALICE THE ELEPHANT

"Wisdom and light express themselves in a wide variety of colors—from the stoic gray fellow who refuses to return your smile to the sunny yellow, tail-wagging puppy who can't love you enough. Behind each is a teaching. If you prefer sunny yellow but you aren't too happy when stoic gray shows up, be curious. What sacred truth is behind blue? Keep going until you can embrace the rainbow."

SARAH

I USED TO RUN INTO A reserved surgeon at the hospital who refused to respond to me, even when I enthusiastically said, "Good morning!" and addressed him by name with my toothy grin. It baffled and annoyed me. What the heck? Then, one day after work, I saw him at the grocery store with his wife and he was talking a blue streak. I was absolutely shocked. I suddenly had the divine insight that he simply couldn't afford to say hello to me, a mere acquaintance. He was saving all of his extra energy for his beloved. I smiled.

Who annoys you? Be curious about why they act the way they do.

Dear God, help me embrace all people and see that they are all, at their center, divine.

MARCH 5

BOUNCE OUT OF BED

ALICE THE ELEPHANT

"Have you ever noticed that a child who has loving parents often bounces out of bed chirping joyfully? If you're finding it difficult to arise in the morning or you awaken stricken with fear, try this practice at night: before you go to bed, ask the Great Power (God, The Universe, or whatever or whomever you pray to) to remove your fear and resistance so you wake feeling kind and excited to be useful. It can make all the difference."

SARAH

FOR ME, RESISTANCE HAS MANY sneaky forms: fighting, judging, worrying, criticizing, arguing, hiding under the covers (despite getting more than enough sleep), complaining, and many other expressions of my fear's greatest hits collection. Of course, if I am grieving, that's different. In grief, I allow myself to be sad and to rest. But for straight up fear, I try to remember that God is the boss of me and to ask to have my resistance banished.

What are you in resistance or fear about today?

Dear God, help me stay close to you so I know there's nothing to fear.

WHAT LOVE CAN DO

ALICE THE ELEPHANT

"Gosh! What can't plants teach you about you? Take one (or three!) under your care and you'll soon learn about what sustains living beings, how much change can happen, and how, like you, they require periodic repotting to allow for expansion. Perhaps most importantly, you'll learn what love can do."

SARAH

I USED TO BE TERRIBLE AT keeping houseplants alive. My husband Mark was the one with the green thumb. I decided to give myself another chance and took a few beautiful plants to my office, where I would be solely responsible for their care. I began to speak kindly to them and water them. I noticed how quickly they grew and what an enormous difference they made. Their presence made the whole space feel more vibrant. As they thrived, my trust in my own abilities grew too.

How could you "re-pot" some part of yourself to expand your possibilities?

Dear God, show me how lean toward the light so I can thrive.

MARCH 7

YOU ARE ENOUGH

ALICE THE ELEPHANT

"You may believe you're too scarred, too old, too unknown, too fat, too flawed, or too hardened to contribute meaningfully. But it's your willingness to be a vessel for perfection that makes the miraculous possible. To witness astonishing beauty passing through weathered, tested, and tenderized beings brings me to my knees."

SARAH

A BEAUTIFUL COLLEAGUE OF MINE, JILL Farmer, laughingly confessed onstage that she had worried, when she accepted the speaking gig, that her butt might be too big. The whole audience laughed at the ridiculousness of this self-assessment and reveled in her willingness to be vulnerable. We all have parts of ourselves that we believe make us unqualified. If I had let all my self-imposed limits rule me, I'd never have written my first book ("I'm too old to master something new like writing / publishing"), led my first retreat ("I'm too unqualified to run a retreat") or shared my first message from Alice ("I'm too imperfect to receive such messages clearly").

What might shift if you were a vessel for astonishing beauty?

Dear God, make me a channel of your love.

WILD AND WISE

ALICE THE ELEPHANT

"If you long to connect with the divine, it will be powerful for you to go out into the wild and find a place where no one will see you—a little hideaway. Lie down and rest. Greet the earth and the sky and request the help you need. Listen and feel for the answers. Of course, you could also ask from right where you are right now. I'm always ready to assist."

SARAH

MY HUSBAND AND I ARRIVED in the big city. We took to the streets, hoping to discover something fun to do or see, but the convention center neighborhood was stark. We felt uninspired, until we stumbled onto a very small park. We lay down in the shade of an old oak tree. We listened to the cicadas' hum. I relaxed and remembered that what I like about cities is their parks and their trees. There is God in those trees.

Go outside today and rest a bit, listening for wisdom.

Dear God, remind me that wisdom is everywhere. Show me how to rest and listen so I may receive it.

MARCH 9

ONWARD

ALICE THE ELEPHANT

*"If overwhelm has you stuck in a quagmire, stop thinking and get into action. Do something—anything—to move toward the big thing. Divine assistance will be activated. When snafus arise, phone a friend for support. Keep going. This is how you get epic sh*t done."*

SARAH

FEELING TERRIBLY STUCK ABOUT HOW to write my first book, I remembered that, while I didn't have a damn clue about how to write a whole book, I could create a file on my laptop for it. I called it "Book Idea" and typed in a few of the thoughts I'd had. That document led to more words and, eventually, I had to find an editor to help me figure out how to organize all the words. As my friend Amitiel's song lyrics go, "Hesitancy can be paralyzing..." Taking action creates momentum. Even the tiniest step counts.

Take one tiny action toward something that feels stuck. Do it within the next hour.

Dear God, keep me out of the quicksand of confusion and resistance. Show me what needs to be done next, and give me the willingness to do it.

YOU ARE NOT THAT

ALICE THE ELEPHANT

"Your mind is always busy thinking, judging, and assessing yourself and everyone around you. But you, thankfully, are not your thoughts. Your highest self is wise, unworried, and knows what's true. All you have to do is listen."

SARAH

THE SHADOW ASPECT OF MY brain / consciousness can be like that scary hyena hidey-hole lair in The Lion King, filled with skeletons and underfed, unethical predators. When I drift there, unaware, my shadow self begins driving the bus. When that happens, my destiny is El Hotel No Bueno. My shadow self thinks things like, That person isn't doing it right, I'm not doing it right, and, Why bother? Nothing matters! Alice often reminds me to meditate, because then I become more skilled at catching myself when I've drifted into the dark place.

How can you reconnect to your wise, eternal self today?

Dear God, help me let unhelpful thoughts go.

MARCH 11

SPEND TIME IN GOOD COMPANY

ALICE THE ELEPHANT

"When I used to be an elephant on Earth, I had many strong emotions: jealousy, fear, anger, and resentment. It was difficult. But I discovered that when I spent time in the company of wise beings I felt better. My grandmother, special aunties, particular trees, and certain watering holes made me feel especially good. In those calm spaces, I felt belonging. I learned to accept my feelings. I learned to forgive myself and others. My love for myself grew and, eventually, I was able to become a calm place for others."

SARAH

MY CHILDHOOD PIANO TEACHER WAS, for me, a sweet oasis in a world of chaos. She exuded a peaceful sensibility that helped me feel more possibilities for myself. I felt stronger just being around her. These days, I have many friends, trees, and special places I can go to when my emotions feel overwhelming.

Who do you reach out to when you need to feel understood?

Dear God, guide me to people and places today that help me grow in self-love and acceptance.

BE TENDER

ALICE THE ELEPHANT

"Taking everything personally can lead to much misery. To avoid this, approach everything softly, like a feather. Walk on the ground like a feather. Listen like a feather. Speak like a feather. Feathers enable flight—not because they are hardened, but because of their softness."

SARAH

BEING A HIGHLY SENSITIVE EMPATHIC person, I often sense the emotions of others (or I think I do). Unfortunately, I can be prone to taking those emotions personally. When Mark would come home from work justifiably exhausted and mildly cranky from a long day of procedures at the hospital, I used to take it as a personal affront. How dare he bring his irritable state into our kitchen? Into our relationship? It took me years to realize that it's not all about me. Feathers taught me that there is great power in softness. Being tender doesn't mean lowering your standards. It simply means softening in the face of hard things.

Where could you try a little tenderness?

Dear God, fill me with tenderness so I can go out into the world with soft ears and eyes.

MARCH 13

#DON'TJUDGE

ALICE THE ELEPHANT

"Judging other people is exhausting and utterly unproductive. When you catch yourself judging, there is a remedy: raise your vibe. Go outside. Pray. Paint. Do anything that helps you feel a little bit (or a lot!) better. From that higher frequency and more formless state, you'll discover that the part of you that wants to criticize has quieted. You might even burst into a guffaw about the way you were thinking about that person before."

SARAH

I'VE WASTED A GOOD BIT of my life being concerned about the behavior, idiosyncrasies, and choices of others. It's done me absolutely no good. My focus on wanting other people to change, takes me out of the game. By judging others I'm playing God. But if I connect with God instead, by being creative or paying Alice a visit, I'm always set straight. Elevated once again, I get back to being productive, calm, and useful to my people.

Who do you wish would change? How could you put the focus back on your relationship with the divine?

Dear God, help me raise my frequency so I can see other people the way you do.

SEE YOU TOO

ALICE THE ELEPHANT

"Consider the hummingbird, how she expands your imagination with her saturated colors, iridescence, agility, and stamina. That she can fly 5000 miles non-stop boggles your mind. You were created by the same Maker. Yet you fail to reckon your own splendor. Look for what's glorious in you too."

SARAH

How many times do I marvel at the amazingness of a spectacular beastie, a friend, or famous person. "Wow! Look what they can do!" Which is often quickly followed by, "I wish I could be like that!" Yet I fail to recognize the marvelous capacities I've been gifted. As I wonder at others' amazing abilities, it's ridiculous not to celebrate and be grateful for the gifts I possess.

What is one of your most stupendous capabilities? How could you use it today to benefit others?

Dear God, let me be an agent of your awesomeness today. Show me how to use the powers you've given me.

MARCH 15

SHARE YOUR BURDENS

ALICE THE ELEPHANT

"Avoid complaining for complaining's sake, but when something bothers you, it's important to share it with another. As long as those conversations seek to find a peaceful solution and the listener can hold your words in confidence, it is good. This is the difference between gossiping and communing."

SARAH

BELIEVING COMPLAINING WAS "BAD," I went through a period when I tried really hard not to complain to my friends about anything. I ended up feeling resentful and frustrated. No wonder! I had bottled up all my dark feelings. Now, when I complain about something, I also try to actively seek a better way to deal with the situation. I understand that it's my way of thinking that's causing my suffering. As I share my conundrum out loud with a friend, I often can hear exactly where I've gone wrong. Or my brilliant friend helps me to an ah-ha! moment.

With every complaint you give voice to today, try to also seek a solution. Be willing to change.

Dear God, help me open to trustworthy friends about my struggles so I may find peace in my heart.

SLOW UP

ALICE THE ELEPHANT

"To discern the difference between an unhelpful yearning and a destiny-fulfilling vision, lie down and get very calm. Surrender physically and ask Mother Earth to hold you. Once you're breathing extremely calmly, consider your desire and ask, 'Is this necessary?' You will hear, sense, or simply know the answer. Although your ego may argue, your soul knows."

SARAH

I WAS HAVING RECURRING FANTASIES OF replacing the 65-year-old metal kitchen cabinets in our 120-year-old house. My mind began to latch onto that idea. We could do it very inexpensively. It would improve the resale value! I lay down and applied Alice's advice. In the calm, when my breath had become so slow it almost stopped, my soul said, This does not need to be done. Let the kitchen cabinets go. In that quiet, I heard something else too: Work on your new book. I realized I'd been scared to work on the fledgling writing project and had been avoiding it like the plague.

Take the time today to get calm and ask about an unclear desire.

Dear God, give me the courage and humility to let go of distracting desires so I can devote myself to the work of my destiny.

MARCH 17

RELAX

ALICE THE ELEPHANT

"If I could give you only one piece of advice for your life, it would be to take it easy. There is a lot to experience, feel, and do, but it will all be more enchanting and less hairy if you can stand down. I believe in you!"

SARAH

ONCE, IN ISTANBUL, I WENT for a Turkish bath with a dear friend, on the recommendation of my mother. The only problem: my mother neglected to tell us we'd be stark naked for the procedure. Being a modest Minnesotan, I was not in my comfort zone. Being enthusiastically scrubbed from stem to stern amid a gathering of other naked people felt quite disturbing. My scrubbing attendant grabbed my stiff leg at one point and fairly shouted in her best English, "Lady, RELAX!" Suddenly, I realized how ridiculously rigid my entire body was, and I decided to try her advice. Turns out, relaxing is the only way to let bliss in.

Try relaxing right now.

Dear God, help me drop all tension from my body and stay restful yet alert so you can work through me.

THINK EXPANSIVELY

ALICE THE ELEPHANT

"Expectations are best when they are great! Expect the very best from yourself and others. And never be disappointed in your performance or others'. Wonder, instead, how it might be better next time. Don't forget that everything is easier when you invoke my supernatural help. Ask. I'll have your back."

SARAH

IT CAN BE TEMPTING FOR me to lower the bar for myself and others to avoid disappointment. Many times, I've dreamed big about my own capabilities, only to believe, afterwards, that I fell short of "the mark." Yet, in each instance like that, I was growing. When I steady myself and allow myself to expand the possibilities (while simultaneously not attaching to them), I'm better prepared to tweak and shift my own contribution.

In what way would you like to raise the bar for yourself?

Dear God, help me raise the bar today, for myself and others, and mindfully evaluate all results through your eyes.

LET THE GOOD TIMES ROLL

ALICE THE ELEPHANT

"When you experience a 'good' thing, we notice that you reflexively begin to fear something terrible is surely coming on its heels. This anxiety is like blinders, blocking all the loveliness. The cure is singing, service, praying, making things, and spending time in good company. Drawing nearer to your Creator will cause an endless upward spiral for you."

SARAH

THIS "WAITING FOR THE OTHER shoe to drop" anxiousness places an upper limit on how sweet I allow life to be. For example, as my beautiful daughter heads off to a formal dance looking truly happy, a dark thought crosses my mind: What if something awful happens tonight, like a car accident, or heartbreak, or worse? As soon as I catch that little fear creeping in, I make a choice to think something different. Grief in life is guaranteed, but I certainly don't want to the one creating it. Why not live like my friend Aviva, an Art Medicine woman, does, by the motto, "After pleasure comes... more pleasure."

Has anxiety stolen the joy of something wonderful in your life? How could you reclaim it?

Dear God, help me allow the good times to roll. Remind me that there is nothing to fear when I keep you close.

MARCH 20

MIND YOUR EDGES

ALICE THE ELEPHANT

"Knowing you can put up or dissolve your boundaries is important. If you choose to dive into the river of someone else's experience, you'll know their pain or their joy. But to be of service to someone who's hurting, you'll need to consciously step out of their river so you can remain untroubled. From this place, you can be of greater assistance. Or, if you're going to dive into their suffering, be damn sure to also swim in their deepest gladness."

SARAH

I USED TO DIVE INTO EXPERIENCING the feelings of whomever I was with, no matter what those feelings were. I got angry as I sat with a friend who was outraged about something. I became afraid when someone spoke of things that frightened them. I had to learn how to connect to the peaceful, untroubled place in myself and remain there. I had to learn to stay untroubled, no matter what, if I wanted to be helpful. Now I have a greater awareness: no matter what anybody is feeling, it is okay.

How could you allow yourself to be compassionate with others without taking on their emotions?

Dear God, help me be present with both the grief and the joy of others.

MARCH 21

WITHOUT CEASING

ALICE THE ELEPHANT

"When you make praying an everyday or even an every hour thing, life gets easier. You begin to see, during these exchanges between you and the Beloved, that you are safe, and there will be a lot more for you to be grateful for. Prayer raises your vibe. Who doesn't need that?"

SARAH

WHEN I WAS GROWING UP, I thought of prayer as something done in church by reading aloud from the 1928 Episcopalian prayer book. Prayer seemed like something foreign, formal, and definitely outside of me. With my own awakening in my forties and the entrance of Alice onto the scene, the sacred began to feel more like family. With my drum, I could connect to the quiet, peaceful, love-filled space where Alice and others resided. Now, having practiced more, I've learned that I don't need to be drumming or in ceremony to pray. Prayer can be an all-day affair (and sometimes it is!). This sweet closeness to the divine is available to me at any time.

How has prayer make your life better?

Dear God, I want to step into closer communion with you. Remind me to pray when I need it most.

MARCH 22

LET IT BE YOU

ALICE THE ELEPHANT

"Misunderstandings between people are common. The more you insist, the worse it gets. Quit reasoning. Pray on the spot. One of you will, hopefully, soften your heart first. For the love of pugs, let it be you."

SARAH

IN THE MIDST OF AN epic sleepover, one of our kids got upset with me. He was in tears, exasperated with me because I wasn't taking his side. I tried to reason with him, but to no avail. The more I reasoned, the more frustrated we both became. Something, thankfully, made me quit and put myself to bed. In bed, I remembered to pray for peace—for him and for me. My heart finally softened and I was able to sleep. In the morning we worked it all out. Arguing with others separates me from the Beloved.

Where in your relationships have you been insisting and reasoning instead of letting the divine handle it?

Dear God, let harmony begin with me.

MARCH 23

WALK WITH CARE

ALICE THE ELEPHANT

"Sometimes you can be a bit of a bull in a china closet. I invite you to pretend that your favorite mouse in the world is always underfoot so you remember to walk tenderly and thoughtfully on this Earth. So many beings are vulnerable. This manner of being will prevent a lot of harm."

SARAH

I TRY TO GO OUT OF my house as Rumi suggests, like a lantern. But sometimes I fail miserably. I behave more like a deranged elephant in musth, aggressively and fearfully lunging about. It doesn't take long before I create real havoc. I forget myself. Seeing everyone as vulnerable reminds to proceed with great care.

What tricks do you use to remember to walk softly in this world?

Dear God, teach me to walk and speak with awareness and care.

MARCH 24

CALL UPON MASTERS

ALICE THE ELEPHANT

"It is good to call upon the masterful spirits who dwell in higher dimensions: Buddha, Jesus, Shiva, Quan Yin, Archangel Gabriel, Ganesha, Mother Mary, Our Lady of Guadalupe and others. They can be of great assistance to you, bringing order and peace to chaos and uncertainty. You have the power to invoke them with your heart and voice."

SARAH

I LOVE THAT WE'VE BEEN GIVEN so many and such diverse divine beings to call upon. From the ample-lapped, grinning Buddha to the ever-embracing Mother Mary, each divine being bears a specific quality each of us needs. I've learned that we need not be Hindu or Buddhist or Catholic to call upon a connection with one of their deities. These masters exist and operate on a level beyond our human limitations, offering solace to anyone who seeks it.

Is there a deity you're curious about? How might you call upon them today?

Dear God, remind me I can call upon powerful beings of light to help myself and others.

MARCH 25

OWN IT

ALICE THE ELEPHANT

"Mushrooms represent a beautiful metaphor for human life. They seemingly burst forth out of nowhere to expand into glorious and utterly unique expressions, only to quickly fade and return back into nothingness. You're in full expansion now, I assure you! What do you want to express on this glorious day you've been given?"

SARAH

ON THE TRAIL NEAR OUR house, I noticed a small mushroom starting to rise out of the ground. I didn't think much about it until the next day when I passed it again and it had quadrupled in size and fairly exploded skyward, tossing chunks of soil aside. Astonished, I kneeled to examine it. I read later that the Ojibwe word for that particular type of mushroom was Puh-pow-we which means the force that pushes things up from the ground.

Have you ever marveled at the creative force? How does the creative force feel to you?

Dear God, help me expand today in ways that honor you.

ALLOW IT ALL

ALICE THE ELEPHANT

"The highs and lows you experience are to be expected. You are made of waves and water. Like the ocean, you're a carrier for energies. Do what you can to allow them to pass through with ease. Sitting tall and breathing is a hell of a tool for doing that."

SARAH

ONE OF THE MOST EXCITING and vulnerable times for me creatively is when I share a new creation. Recently, I invited people to experience a new retreat I had conceived of. It involved facing death in order to live more deeply. Rather than filling quickly, the class had only a single person registered in the first month. My dying-to-live idea wasn't (apparently) a welcome one. That was tough, because I'd thought everybody would love it. After some deep soul-searching, I realized that sort of retreat might not be for everybody. It was pretty radical. It might take some time to fill the retreat, but that didn't mean it wasn't good work for me to do.

Is something not working for you at the moment? Would you be willing to give whatever that is three deep breaths?

Dear God, teach me how to let the waves of energy, feeling, and thought pass through me with ease.

MARCH 27

FROLIC

ALICE THE ELEPHANT

"Learn to relish being in the not-knowing place. Enjoy the free fall. Revel in it! This is real power."

SARAH

I REMEMBER HOW I ONCE GOT so nervous about how people might perceive some creative writing I'd done. Full of anxiety, I went to Alice for wisdom. In the spirit reality where we met, she took me on a leap into the "unknown," sans parachutes. It was terrifying—until I looked over at Alice. She was doing somersaults, enjoying herself immensely. Her attitude made my inner control freak giggle a little at herself.

How could you release your attachment to outcomes and have a little fun instead?

Dear God, I put all my worries about outcomes in your hands so I can be at peace.

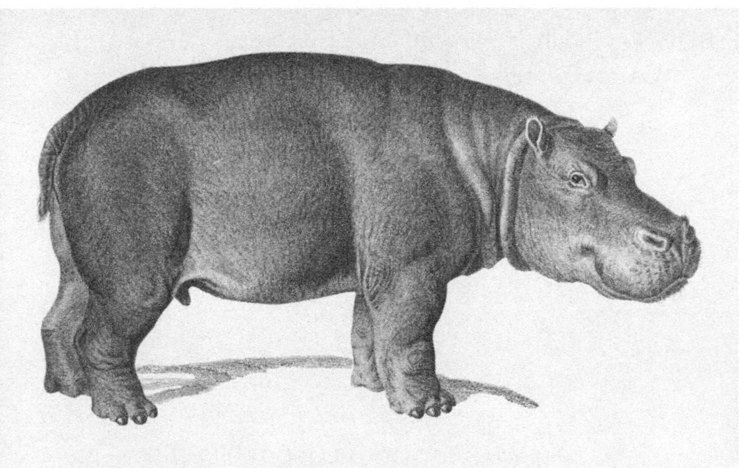

WE ARE FAMILY

ALICE THE ELEPHANT

"I can't overemphasize how important it is to get along. Remembering that you're all harmonious at the level of the soul helps. Each of you craves love and belonging, but you're so afraid to let each other in! Caring about one another is the first step."

SARAH

When I began my formal spiritual training, our teacher admonished us to remember that, underneath all our personalities and uniqueness, we're all divinely in agreement. She admonished us to not get caught up in reacting to each other and judging. Whenever I begin a retreat, I tell my participants the same thing. It makes all the difference.

Who do you need to see more deeply at the soul level?

Dear God, help me remember that we are all related. We are all family.

MARCH 29

DO WHAT IT TAKES

ALICE THE ELEPHANT

"I never promised it would be easy to grow in compassion. You say you want to help, but are you willing to do what it takes to become one who can be truly helpful? It's not easy, but it's definitely a worthy road to travel."

SARAH

A WISE SHAMAN I CONSIDER A teacher had a single desire when he was growing up: "I just wanted to be a helper." Years later, he found himself in the Amazon jungle, naked, crazed, rolling in the mud. His spiritual teacher had given him a large cup of Ayahuasca, a brew made of medicinal plants, to drink so he could be initiated into shamanic wisdom. "I just want to go home!" he cried in anguish. Eventually, the medicine's effects subsided. The next morning, his teacher said, "You must drink the medicine again tonight." My teacher couldn't believe it! He said, "All I wanted was to be a helper!" Of course, in the end, he did continue with his training. He continued to be willing to drink the medicine, which helped him to learn and to grow his abilities to be a helper.

What will you do today to face the difficult tasks on your spiritual path?

Dear God, teach me what I need to learn. I am willing.

MARCH 30

KEEP THE FAITH

ALICE THE ELEPHANT

"Sometimes, just before the miracle is made possible, you give up (spirit pachydermal face plant). If you could just hang in there one minute longer, be willing to take action one more time, an entire world of possibilities would open to you. Keep the everloving faith!"

SARAH

FOR YEARS, I HAD BEEN praying for a shift in our marriage. But, time after time, a feeling of separation would arise between me and my husband Mark, like an impenetrable wall. We loved each other, don't get me wrong, but we didn't consistently experience the tender closeness we both yearned for. When a fresh opportunity came for healing the relationship, I could see that it was up to me to be vulnerable and profess my love. A cynical part of me balked Really? I've done that before. Nothing will ever change. Another part calmly said, Say it again. Express your love again. That day, a miracle occurred and since then everything has been sweeter between us. Not perfect, but the tender closeness is with us.

In what ways do you or could you keep the faith that a miracle is possible?

Dear God, remind me that things happen with your timing, not mine.

MARCH 31

USE CURIOSITY

ALICE THE ELEPHANT

"Approach every experience with great curiosity. Wonder why you have been called here, to this place, to meet with these people, to hear this song, or to see this image. Not only will this make each day a wild adventure, you won't miss the absolute magnificence being created on your behalf."

SARAH

I HAD SIGNED UP FOR A course taking place across the country. My friend and roomie-to-be had to bail out because of life circumstances. I almost canceled too, but remembered the strong conviction I had originally felt when registering. On the first day, I felt baffled, because none of the course seemed particularly helpful. I even felt mildly resentful. But then, on day two, something happened I could not have predicted. Life-changing words flashed on the presenter's screen, and I met someone. Both incidents helped me transform one of the greatest challenges of my life.

What are you curious about? How could you turn an obligation into an adventure?

Dear God, remind that there are no accidents. Everything is conspiring to help me.

April

APRIL 1

EVERYTHING IS SACRED

ALICE THE ELEPHANT

"When you begin accepting that everything is sacred, you get closer to the truth. All the denial you continually issue drains your life force and halts your progress."

SARAH

I COULD ACCEPT THAT THE THINGS I deemed "good" were acceptable: flowers, nicely behaved people, gratitude, etc. But…, my helping spirits challenged me, what about death, human waste (literal and figurative!), child pornography, addiction... and all the other stuff you don't want to look at? When you can accept that all of that is also a part of this sacred world, Sarah, you'll be better off." I began to understand that I didn't have to like all things, but by negating them, I ran the risk of not embracing all of my own, flawed self too. I didn't need to disavow my shadow side (or that of the collective), but, instead, I needed to acknowledge it so it wouldn't get the best of me.

Where are you jealous, or what perturbs you, or how do you want to manipulate something or someone? Embrace this as part of your humanness.

Dear God, help me be conscious and accepting of my own shadow.

APRIL 2

LET GO AND BE CARRIED

ALICE THE ELEPHANT

"Confidence is not a product of the self. It grows from the experiences you have when you let go (out of exasperation or by choice) of the reins and discover that something much greater carries you. When you begin to rely more on this type of backing, you become confident. You are confidence."

SARAH

When I began teaching workshops and giving talks, I got horribly nervous. I'd frantically burn incense, commence sage-ing the hell out of myself, my computer, everything, thinking to myself, "It's all on me!" It has taken me a long time to realize that things go a lot better when I call upon my loving and compassionate spirits and ask them to support me in my work. I've realized it's them, not me, who does the heavy lifting (if any is required). At some point, I began to relax and enjoy these events much more. I was able to relax and trust. I experienced confidence.

If you're worried about something, how could you call upon whomever you pray to and ask them to be with you during this time?

Dear God, I put my trust in you today. I'll do my part the best way I know how.

APRIL 3

BE VULNERABLE

ALICE THE ELEPHANT

"Whenever you are irritated by a loved one, try offering yourself extreme self-care. Tend to the places in you that hurt. Remind yourself it's okay to be needy. Only then will you be able to be compassionate with another."

SARAH

A DEAR FRIEND AND I DIDN'T see eye to eye on something and I was so disappointed. Why didn't this thing work for her too? I longed for agreement between us, but knew if I was trying to change her, I was on shaky ground. I asked Alice how I could be more compassionate with her and better understand her viewpoint. Alice gave me the message above. Turning toward myself, I discovered that my heart was bruised. Before expecting myself to be the Dalai Lama, it was my job to give myself what I needed.

Take the time to be compassionate with yourself today.

Dear God, let me be compassionate with myself so I can be more compassionate with those I love.

HONOR YOUR GRIEF

ALICE THE ELEPHANT

"When you feel overwhelmed by grief, it can be difficult to find joy. You worry that you should stop feeling sad. But your power is in your broken heart. To grieve properly is to have loved deeply."

SARAH

TO BRING MORE JOY INTO my life, I committed to dance every day for a year. When I began boogying down daily, it felt wild and wonderful. A few weeks later, my mom was diagnosed with lung cancer and I suddenly discovered that I couldn't dance the same way anymore. A wave of grief engulfed me. It was so hard to see Mom feeling shaken, and to think about the possibility of losing her. My heart ached. To top it off, I felt guilty about my grief. I didn't want my grief to bring others down. Then Alice reminded me that grief is a privilege and it's how we honor the love we've received. So I danced my grief.

Do you give yourself permission to grieve? How might you express your feelings today?

Dear God, help me to honor my grief whenever it occurs.

APRIL 5

YOU'VE GOT THIS

ALICE THE ELEPHANT

"Stop doubting. For pug's sake, trust!"

SARAH

AT AGE FORTY-TWO, WHEN I suddenly had the urge to begin writing books, learn about shamanic healing, and discover a new vocation, I wanted guarantees. I wanted assurance that if I worked hard my new career would support our family financially or, at the very least, my work would be well received. I kept visiting Alice to ask for promises. "Help!" I'd cry to her. "How can I be sure that this book will be any good?" and "How can I be sure this retreat I'm planning is a good idea?" Alice always smiled indulgently and reminded me to stop doubting.

How would you proceed today if you kicked doubt to the curb?

Dear God, I surrender everything I do to you.

ONE OF A KIND

ALICE THE ELEPHANT

"Never compare your family (chosen or otherwise) with another person's family. Yours is precious in its own way."

SARAH

A FRIEND AND HIS FAMILY GO on amazing camping adventures. They kayak and canoe together. They hiked in New Zealand. Every time I saw photos of that smiling family, I would droop slightly, thinking, I wish we did that. It isn't that our family hasn't traveled and camped together. We have! But sometimes those trips weren't the easiest. I wondered if, somehow, we had done a bad job as parents. Was that why our family togetherness didn't look like that other family's? Alice reminded me to see the beauty and profound specialness of our family—our humor, our shared love of pugs, our care and concern for each other, and, most of all, our mutual respect of our extreme differences (okay—most of the time!). I wept with joy thinking about my family like that, and I refused to ever compare us again.

What is beautiful about your family (chosen or otherwise)?

Dear God, keep me from comparing and despairing so I can be present with my chosen people.

SHARE YOUR MEDICINE

ALICE THE ELEPHANT

"Do what you're fucking amazing at. Give us what you've got!"

SARAH

WHAT WE "SHOULD" BE DOING can be confusing for many of us artist and healer types. At first, we may have little understanding of what our secret sauce—our God-given superpowers—are. Or we dismiss the things we're really great at. For example, I used to think my ability to throw parties or whip up great meals from an empty fridge was no big deal. Doesn't everybody do that? Not everybody can do what you do. If you're not sure, ask a few friends the question, "What am I amazing at?" and be prepared to be astonished by what you hear. Then do more of those things! This is medicine for all. Tell your friends what their superpowers are too.

Name one of your superpowers and find a way to use it today.

Dear God, remind me of the things I do really well. Help me share the gifts you've given me.

GO FOR BROKE

ALICE THE ELEPHANT

"Go big. Dream in absurd and ridiculous directions. That's where the magic is, dagnabbit. Dream big, then take little, feelgood steps toward the magic."

SARAH

I HAD FINISHED MY LIFE COACH training and learned enough about shamanism to be helping myself when somebody asked me, "What would you do if you knew you could not fail?" I must have been feeling expansive that day because I answered, "Well, I'd create a retreat in Hawaii with some other coaches, and I'd teach people how to go on a shamanic journey to meet their own spirit animals!" In reality, those felt like huge leaps. I wasn't a travel agent. Heck, I'd never attended a spiritual retreat, much less gone to one across the ocean, much less led one. Yet, with intention, one thing led to another and, six months later, I was in Hawaii helping to put on such a retreat. Had I been logical, I would have talked myself out of it.

What would be really amazing to do or experience? If you knew you couldn't fail, what step would you take toward that experience today?

Dear God, remind me that, with you, even the ridiculous can become possible.

APRIL 9

REDUCE

ALICE THE ELEPHANT

"Commit to very little. Devote yourself to three things or projects you consider most important. This will save a lot of trouble Then surrender to the fact that you will deviate from there."

SARAH

I WASN'T DIAGNOSED WITH ADHD UNTIL my early forties. What a relief it was to discover why I'd always thought about things differently. It also made me realize I'd been gleefully (and sometimes not so gleefully) "scattering my energies" since 1967. One of the perspectives that helped me most was what Alice shared above: focusing on a few things at a time. An "I want to do everything all the time" program overwhelmed me. I love new ideas and fresh starts, but finishing can feel excruciating. So I try to be cautious about pointing myself in too many different directions at once. Some days it still happens, but usually I can quickly refocus.

What three things feel most important for you to focus on?

Dear God, help me commit only to the most important things you want me to work on so that I can do them well.

APRIL 10

LIGHTEN UP

ALICE THE ELEPHANT

"Permit yourself occasional lionish bouts of moodiness, but never lose track of your precious inner jackass."

SARAH

ONE DAY, WHILE TRAVELING WITH a friend, she asked me what was wrong. "Where did Sunny Sarah go?" she asked. Nobody had ever asked me that. I'd awakened stressed and cranky and, apparently, I wasn't hiding it well. I suddenly felt embarrassed that I couldn't manage to be sunny all the time. I'd disappointed her. Now I realize it's just part of the deal to be cranky sometimes, and that's okay. For me, crankiness very often indicates that I need to breathe and take myself a little less seriously.

Is there some way you're taking yourself too seriously?

Dear God, connect me to my sense of humor so I take myself a little less seriously.

APRIL 11

YOU WERE BORN TO FREAK

ALICE THE ELEPHANT

"Embrace the fact that not everybody will 'get' you. You were born to restore balance to the world by expressing your freaky uniqueness. All the goodness you have to share is not for everybody, but it is for a very special group of people: your people."

SARAH

When I'm advising humans who are embarking on publicly sharing their art, music, writing, or a new therapeutic skill, I suggest that they identify who their service or creation is for. "It's for everybody!" they cry, as I once did. But if we try to make something for everybody, its potency is likely to be diluted. Imagine writing a letter to this person you adore who is hurting. Who is this person? What do they need to see, hear, or know from you? Tell them rather than telling everyone. That one person is one of "your people." There are more!

Are you trying to be everything to everybody with your work? Who is your creation really for?

Dear God, show me how to express my freaky inner multitudes in the way you designed me to.

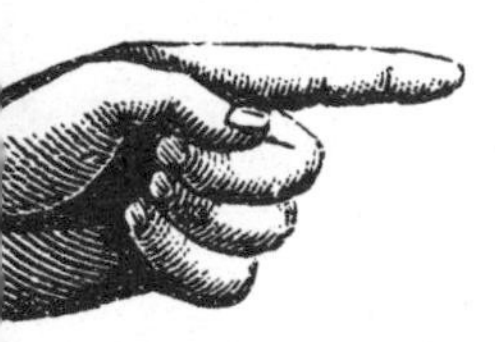

For further exploration, please see my book *Born to FREAK: A Salty Primer for Irrepressible Humans.*

BEFRIEND YOUR BODY

ALICE THE ELEPHANT

"Be good to yourself. It's not easy to do and be all the things you long to be here on Earth, so make time for breaks. Be sure you get enough sleep. Tend to your health. Nobody but you can take those medicinal steps, so take them."

SARAH

NAIVE AND THRILLED ABOUT MY second publishing deal, I agreed to a book contract that required me to write a 100,000-word book in less than three months. It meant working seven days a week and getting up at 5:00 a.m. for three months straight, in addition to my otherwise full schedule. I only took a few days off. My body suffered from the extended hours of sitting in a chair (and the reduced exercise), and my relationships suffered. As my son Charlie aptly put it, "You were kind of crabby that winter." I was the one who had said yes to such a timeline. Now I know that, in the future, I can make different choices.

How could you find a balance between productivity and self-care today?

Dear God, help me plan my work schedule and projects without sacrificing my wellbeing.

APRIL 13

CHOOSE WISELY

ALICE THE ELEPHANT

"Imagine the vast Universe, with all of its planets, stars, and galaxies. You are but a minuscule part of it, and yet you are not insignificant! Your contribution matters. What part do you want to play? What would bring you the deepest contentment? Do that!"

SARAH

For nearly twenty years, I practiced as a physician in a hospital setting. As a pathologist, I was paid to hunt for disease. The work fascinated me for almost twenty years... until it didn't. Suddenly, something beyond my control began to change me. I became fascinated by a new question: "What makes people well?" It was a confusing time. It took me a few years to realize that the new part I wanted to play was being someone who helped others create health and vitality.

Are you pleased with the role you currently play in the Universe? If not, what role might feel better?

Dear God, point me toward my North Star. Direct me to my work here on Earth.

APRIL 14

GIVE AND TAKE

ALICE THE ELEPHANT

"Everything that is, is alive: your home, your car, each thing you possess. It's good to cherish this aliveness. Ask the spirit of your home to tell you how it would like to be honored. Do your best to show your respect and gratitude by complying with its requests. Observe how the spaces and things sing back to you with thanks for your support. Reciprocity is a treasure to experience."

SARAH

HOMES HAVE ALWAYS BEEN A deep love of mine. I enjoy creating them and discovering how others live in theirs. I've noticed that when I neglect our spaces, I feel discontent. Clutter builds up or the arrangement of furniture feels stale. Taking a bit of time to tend to the house, expressing my gratitude as I go, makes a huge difference.

How does the spirit of your home wish to be honored by you?

Dear God, thank you for this shelter you've provided us. Help me honor it by listening to what it needs and tending to it.

APRIL 15

OFFLOAD

ALICE THE ELEPHANT

"Imagine us lowering from the heavens an amazing serving tray made of ornate sterling silver. This is for you to pile your troubles, worries, and concerns onto. Let us take these burdens up and away from you."

SARAH

MY INNER CONTROL FREAK IS stronger on some days. I worry about so much that it's hard to catalog all the fears! My ego doesn't like this or that. She has a solution! She's got it figured out. She will control everything and everyone to keep me (or my loved ones) safe. But it all works so much better when I do as Alice suggests: give it all up and humbly ask for suggestions.

What situation or person do you need to put on that heavenly silver tray right now?

Dear God, I give you everything today and quietly await your instructions.

ASK

ALICE THE ELEPHANT

"Many of you are baffled and confused about how to pray. One simple way is to find a quiet place to sit, and then ask the divine (the Universe, Beloved, God... whomever you'd like to pray to) to enter you. This may take some practice, but you'll soon come to know the sweet feeling of being enveloped by a tender blanket of peace. It's simple. Don't complicate it."

SARAH

YEARS AGO, I HAD A rather harrowing encounter with spirit. I sensed that God was omnipotent and it terrified me. I laughed in that moment, mildly horrified at my past efforts at controlling my life. I bowed my head and begged the great force, "Teach me how to pray!" I immediately received an assignment to go to my mother and ask her to teach me how to pray. Mom's method was very simple: 1) speak to God as if he's a friend, 2) express your gratitude, and 3) ask for help where you need it. I had always thought praying needed to be much more mysterious and complex than that.

How do you like to pray?

Dear God, please teach me how to pray.

APRIL 17

GET DOWN ON IT

ALICE THE ELEPHANT

"Your body is designed to dance. We encourage you to use this ability every day. Even if you're bed-bound, you may be able to use your hands and fingers to dance with dust particles waltzing through sunlight. Each time you move expressively, it strengthens your relationship to the entire cosmos. Movement is a prayer too."

SARAH

ONE OF MY TEACHERS TOOK me into a ceremony with others. She called spirits that were unknown to us and invited us to allow them to enter and dance us. The whole idea scared me a bit. I didn't want to feel "out of control." For two years I watched my fellow students allow themselves to be danced by apparently friendly (but unknown) spirits. I was in awe of their joy. Finally, one year, I let go and allowed myself to be danced. It was a great honor. When our dance was over, I felt much freer. There had been nothing to fear.

What song would be fun for you to dance to today for a few minutes?

Dear God, let's dance!

PRIMP

ALICE THE ELEPHANT

"Make yourself as beautiful or as dashing as you can be. You are the canvas! Awesomely adorn yourself in any way you please: mutton-chop sideburns, smoky eyes, or an otherworldly shag. It pleases the Creator when you express your signature style, and it uplifts everyone around you."

SARAH

I USED TO WORRY THAT WEARING make-up was superficial. It seemed frivolous or egoic to beautify myself. That was what I told myself as I quickly threw my hair into a ponytail every day, believing my appearance probably didn't really matter. Slowly, with Alice's help, I've learned that taking the time to present myself in the best way is also sacred work. And there are no rules. I can go full "Dolly Parton" and wear a wig and a full face of make-up, or I can go naked-faced and natural. As long as I take the time to tend to my appearance, it's all good. I feel better when I give my appearance some attention.

What could you do to your appearance to reflect the beauty of Creation?

Dear God, I want to shine for you today. Show me how!

SIT

ALICE THE ELEPHANT

"You humans are always talking about needing to find a balance. What I want to suggest to you is that the circumstances of your life will probably never feel perfectly balanced. But what you can do is find a powerful equilibrium inside yourself. This sort of balance is definitely attainable. It begins with taking long, slow, deep breaths and adding a boatload of awareness. Meditation is truly magnificent for developing this state."

SARAH

A SEASON OF BUSYNESS DESCENDS AND I realize the next few weekends will involve speaking gigs, writing, and workshops. Suddenly, I'm overwhelmed. Why did I say I would do all of this? Then I remember that I don't have to do it all right now. I only have to prepare for whatever is next. And breathe.

How is your breathing at this moment?

Dear God, give me the willingness to sit in stillness so I may develop more equanimity.

APRIL 20

MAKE LIGHT

ALICE THE ELEPHANT

"Don't neglect humor. When you find a fantastically funny YouTube video, text it to everybody you love. Make time to regale people with the ridiculous things your kid, dog, or pet rabbit did. Let no whoopee cushion gather dust! This is a powerful medicine."

SARAH

MY PHONE ALARM PROBABLY RINGS nine times a day to remind or re-remind me of something I need to do or a dentist appointment I need to take a kid to. I have a daily "habit stack" of reminders that includes meditation and other spiritual work, but I've noticed I have no regular commitment to humor. I'm changing that! Blessed is the friend who tags you about a Saturday Night Live video you need to see. My son Charlie often hides behind walls to jump out and surprise me, which always makes us laugh really hard.

Whose funny bone could you tickle today?

Dear God, open me to sources of comedy in my daily life to help me stay buoyant.

APRIL 21

DON'T STOP BELIEVIN'

ALICE THE ELEPHANT

"Do you have a habit you'd like to break? There's always a way. Never give up on yourself! Engage with others who have already figured it out. Ask for my help. In time, you'll be able to change your behavior in ways you'd never dreamed possible."

SARAH

I HAVE BEEN A LIFETIME OFFENDER at nail-biting. It began as thumb-sucking. I've tried everything to break the habit. Awful-tasting nail polish. Fake nails. Regular manicures. Gum-chewing. You name it. Nothing worked, but I didn't give up. At age fifty-two, with some help from an online community that deeply understood biters like me (it turned out I was a "meat grinder" subtype), and support from my friend Suzi, I finally kicked this habit. When I look at my nails now I feel a gentle pride. That self-destructive habit only took me 52 years to conquer. It's never too late.

Do you have any habits you'd like to be rid of? Who could help you?

Dear God, lend me the strength to fix this unhelpful pattern in my life. I can't do it without you.

APRIL 22

STOP

ALICE THE ELEPHANT

"Be aware that, after a certain number of hours, your creative productivity takes a nosedive. It's prudent to quit while you're ahead. Calmly put down the paintbrush. It takes discipline to place the period at the end of a sentence and leave the desk, to wrap up your project for now, somehow. Then go play. Refresh, get social, move your body, make soup, visit somebody who's lonely so you can be unlonely together. Tomorrow you'll be able to come back refreshed."

SARAH

Once I get rolling on a creative tear, I can be like the average three-year-old kid who you need to warn several times before you leave the playground that "We will need to be going soon," or they'll have a tantrum. My creative window is about four to five hours before I begin to fade. I've learned that Alice is right: I have to stop before I really want to. There is discipline to this creative work.

What happens to you if you push beyond your natural quitting time?

Dear God, help me remember that my creative work is not a sprint but a marathon.

APRIL 23

BRING HEAVEN HERE

ALICE THE ELEPHANT

"Hugging is spiritual training. Try to give and get as many hugs as you can. I suggest twenty per day. If you find yourself in solitary confinement, you'll need to imagine 20 warm embraces every day. Every hug brings you closer to us and prepares you for the galactic bear hug we'll give you when you return home."

SARAH

When I first met my helping spirits, Mother Bear and Alice, one of the sweetest parts of our visits was the hugs they gave me. I was a bit hug-starved at the time. Working too many hours, being incredibly busy with little kids, I rarely seemed to run into other people much. If I did, I didn't know to hug them. Now I'll hug anybody with a pulse! I try to remember to ask first. Hugs, to me, are heaven.

Have you gotten and given enough hugs today? Who else could you hug?

Dear God, help me find appropriate hug recipients and show me how to be good at it.

NO-LIMIT MIND

ALICE THE ELEPHANT

"Claim your unsinkable nature. Say it out loud! With my help, there's nothing you can't do. Kick doubt, indecision, and cynicism to the curb. Be grateful to Source for any and all results."

SARAH

NEUROSCIENCE TEACHES US THAT THE words we choose can impact our outcomes. The difference between saying, "I can't eat sugar" and "I don't eat sugar" is that you're more likely to be able to stay in integrity with the latter statement (if not eating sugar is what you want). That's because "don't" affirms your identity as a person who can choose. If you want to be buoyant and resilient, choose to be unsinkable. Say it with me: "I am unsinkable!"

What new identity do you want to claim? Say, "I am the kind of person who..." and end the statement with the behavior you choose.

Dear God, thank you for the power of words. With you I can do great things!

JOLT YOURSELF

ALICE THE ELEPHANT

"Plunge into cold water often. Or do anything similarly uncomfortable on the daily. This temporary discomfort you experience is a medicine that prepares you for vital creative expansion. Avoiding the uncomfortable will ultimately keep you from your feelgood. The exhilaration will be worth it!"

SARAH

In the summer, when it was time for a swim, my dad and I had radically different approaches to the cold lake. He would run, whooping and yelling, off the dock and plunge straight in, cannonball style. For years, I preferred the slow immersion method: painstakingly acclimating to the frigid water, starting at the shinbone, then up to my waist (the worst!), then finally my head. It was rather exhausting. One day I decided to try my dad's method and simply leaped, without complication, off the end of the dock. So much faster and better. One of my favorite shamans swears by her daily freezing cold shower. I'm going to try one tomorrow.

What would you be willing to do today that's uncomfortable, to grow your willingness to be uncomfortable in service of your creativity?

Dear God, take away my resistance to life and growth.

LOVE IS HERE TOO

ALICE THE ELEPHANT

"The same intelligence, love, compassion, harmoniousness, tenderness, and peace is hidden behind every person, place, and thing. You don't ever have to go anywhere but here to know it."

SARAH

THERE WAS A PERIOD WHEN I was particularly concerned about a certain political figure. I worried quite a bit about the damage that person might wreak. It was on my mind when I entered a ceremony. Suddenly, in the middle of the meditation, a thought popped in: That political person I'm thinking about is a lightworker too! What?! My logical mind fought that idea for a good while. But the divine insight was that he too was around, in his own way, to help us all grow and expand. I thought of him as a tiny, helpless infant for a while, until I saw his innocence and human-ness. That day, I realized that, while I may not like the behavior of some people, they too are made from the same Source. We are all family. We cannot escape this.

Who do you need to see as human, just like you? Can you imagine them as a helpless infant?

Dear God, help me see everyone as family.

APRIL 27

SEE

ALICE THE ELEPHANT

"Look into people's eyes. There you will sense worlds upon worlds. The depth may scare you and you may want to look away, but don't. This is only fear of yourself and of the other. Look with all your heart. This is how to know one another."

SARAH

AT A TRANSFORMATIONAL RETREAT ONCE, we were invited to look into each other's eyes for a sustained period—a few minutes or so. It was a strange and very moving experiment. At first it felt awkward, but then tears came to my eyes. I had immense compassion for the beautiful person I saw behind those eyes. I remember that when the exercise was over, I looked up and so many people were blowing their noses and wiping their eyes. We had all been strangers before that.

How do you feel when somebody makes a lot of eye contact with you? Does it depend on the person?

Dear God, give me the courage to encounter myself and others with my eyes.

APRIL 28

SACRED FAMILY

ALICE THE ELEPHANT

"We spirit animals and spirit helpers in human form are friends and family of the highest order. We're here to help you balance the challenges of physicality with love and compassion. We are a gift from the Creator—your personal supernatural champions. Every human can benefit from joining forces with one of us."

SARAH

I HAVE EXPERIENCED THE LOVE AND compassion of the beasties making me come alive. When people who struggle with their purpose or who feel disempowered ask me what I recommend, I always say, "Would you be interested in meeting a spirit animal?" My beastie relationships are the most life-changing non-human friendships I've ever had. While spirit animals may sound avant-garde, they can be providers of extremely pragmatic advice (as this book demonstrates).

Do you have a spirit animal you call your own? How have they helped you?

Dear God, thank you for giving us the spirits of the beasties who lovingly guide and protect us.

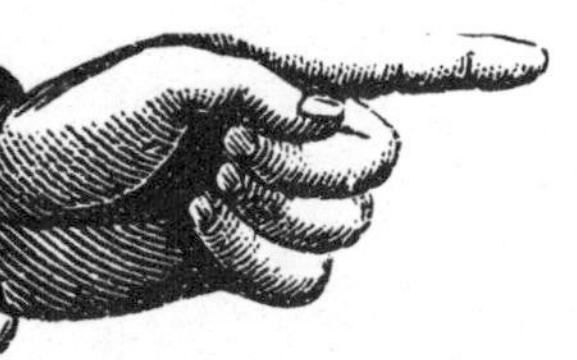

GO TO FOLLOWYOURFEELGOOD.COM/DISCOVER-YOUR-CORE-BEASTIE TO GET ACCESS TO A GUIDED MEDITATION TO FIND YOURS.

APRIL 29

LOVE THE WEATHER

ALICE

"When you catch yourself carping about the weather I gently suggest that you cease and desist. Embrace the cold rain, the overwhelming heat, the blizzard, and the dark clouds. Soak up the immense beauty of this infinite variety."

SARAH

SO MANY FORMS OF RESISTANCE! Although I've heard Alice's good advice about weather before, just today I responded to clouds and fog with, "Boy, it's gloomy out, isn't it?" What if, instead of proclaiming it gloomy, I celebrated the bright contrast of coral-colored fall leaves against the darker skies, or the way fog softens things and makes it all so mysterious. All of this is an ongoing, endlessly creative show for us. Thank you!

For today, refuse to join conversations that center on weather complaints. Smile instead.

Dear God, help me see weather and its immense beauty as you see it.

WHY WAIT?

ALICE THE ELEPHANT

"If you're able to feel righteous anger in yourself and sense despair in another, you are also eminently qualified to perceive the divine. You only need to sit in silence and ask it to draw near. This great power can't wait to hold you in its magnificent tenderness. Waiting is for suckers."

SARAH

EVEN IF I'M IN A temporary moat of gloom about my own life circumstances, or feeling sad about something that's happening for another human, all I need to do is shift toward that great power that never fails me. I can opt for meditation or a more personal one-on-one visit with Alice or one of the other helping spirits. Spirit is always here for me. All I need to do is ask.

Do you believe in your ability to open a channel to the divine? How often do you open it?

Dear God, I know I'm designed to be able to connect with you. Help me remember this when I am struggling.

May

HIT PAUSE

ALICE THE ELEPHANT

"Avoid taking action when you feel moody or otherwise discombobulated. Find your feelgood first. Acting from that place will be most beneficial."

SARAH

HAVE YOU EVER IMPULSIVELY POSTED on social media or said something to a loved one and then moments or hours later wished you could retract it? When I do that, it's usually because the words came from a self-righteous, mildly cranky, or other uninspired way of thinking. Feel good first, then take action. And you always have permission to be human. We never get it right one hundred percent of the time.

In what area of your life might you need to be more aware of your feelings before you take action?

Dear God, help me pause when I'm about to express or act from a non-peaceful place.

MAY 2

INVENT

ALICE THE ELEPHANT

"Close your eyes and imagine a super-sacred circle of immense beauty around you. Fill it with flowers, divine patterns, scents, and whatever else feels good to you. Bask in that beauty. Sense it behind you, before you, beneath you, below you, and on either side of you. This is just one way to shift your frequency."

SARAH

I LOVE WHAT ALICE SUGGESTS. THE power of our imagination to invisibly alter our experience is big. And it doesn't stop there. When I was visiting one of my favorite elders in Peru, she explained to me that she believes we can be masters of shifting energy. With a few simple tools—a candle, music, an open window—we can change the entire atmosphere for ourselves and those who enter our space.

How do you like to shift the energy in your home or at work? What other ways might you like to try?

Dear God, give me awareness to know when energy needs to be shifted and inspiration about how to shift it.

MAY 3

FOLLOW

ALICE THE ELEPHANT

"Imagine the Creator is your dance partner. You don't want to be all herky-jerky and try to lead this immense force around the dance floor, do you? No, you're wiser than that. Be light on your feet and tune in to the one who's leading you. Everything is so much easier when you allow yourself to be led."

SARAH

ACCORDING TO MY BELOVED HUSBAND Mark, I'm a rather inept dance partner because I like to lead. He's right. This fun fact makes me aware that I may also have that pattern elsewhere in my life. I've been working with this sacred dancing with the divine that Alice suggests as I plan workshops and ceremonies. I always have a plan in place, but I've become more willing to soften and let what wants to happen occur (instead of strictly sticking to my plan). This has brought a lot more ease and enjoyment for everybody.

Are you tuned in to your divine partner? How would it feel to be led?

Dear God, I am here on your awesome dance floor and ready to be led today.

MAY 4

WELL, HELLO

ALICE THE ELEPHANT

"The Irish say there's a pot of gold at the end of every rainbow because rainbows are wake-up calls. They remind you of the immense beauty of the Earth. This beauty—that's in every direction you look—is the treasure."

SARAH

ONE GREAT BOON OF SOCIAL media is that I catch so many more rainbows. Rainbows stop us in our tracks. And we can't seem to keep them to ourselves. We share them compulsively. According to a lot of wise people I know, special rainbows, like circular (whirling) or double rainbows, bring even more "wake up" with them and often act as synchronistic messages confirming we're on the right track.

When you see a rainbow, what do you think it means?

Dear God, help me pay attention to all the amazing beauty you have put in front of me today.

MAY 5

PILGRIMAGE

ALICE THE ELEPHANT

"When you feel drawn to certain locations, there is a reason. Certain spots can efficiently teach you what you need to learn. Follow the pull of those places. A sense of being called somewhere is a good thing to explore."

SARAH

AFTER WATCHING THE FILM GANDHI in high school, I longed to visit India. That great man and his equanimity really left an impression on me. I wasn't totally sure why I needed to go to India so badly, but I went. My visit taught me enormous things about myself, the power of spirit in certain places, and prayer. I've also felt drawn to places closer to home, like the tiny, local stream I visit over and over again. That place has also become a powerful teacher about life, and I carry those lessons with me always.

Do you feel drawn to any special places? Have you heeded their call?

Dear God, help me find a way to visit the special places that call to me so I can unfold their mystery.

MAY 6

HOW TO HELP

ALICE THE ELEPHANT

"Success is the deeply comforting and contented feeling that comes from being in service to Creation in a satisfying way. It only comes after experimentation, failure, and adjustments. One secret shortcut is to dedicate all your actions to the divine."

SARAH

On my first retreat, which I launched with some friends, I remember dreading shopping for breakfast groceries. We planned to feed the participants a simple buffet breakfast each morning. I disliked grocery shopping. That chore reminded me of the overwhelm of home. More grocery shopping wasn't what I wanted to create in my new life. When it dawned on me that I was grocery shopping to be of service to the retreat participants (and ultimately, Spirit!), it suddenly became easier. These days, I try to plan retreats that don't require me to grocery shop. I also remind myself that I am just a servant here.

Do you feel content? What actions could you dedicate to the divine?

Dear God, I am at your service.

MAY 7

SERENITY NOW

ALICE THE ELEPHANT

"If you find yourself desperately wanting someone you care about to seek help or healing for themselves, you're in trouble. Trust that, just like you, that person has a direct line to the divine. Love them hard, but let them be."

SARAH

OH BOY. FOR ME, ALICE'S advice is harder than it looks. Especially if the person in question is somebody I love dearly. I have had to learn, through the school of hard knocks and twelve-step recovery programs, that I don't get to play God in other people's lives. The person I love is much more likely to be helped by me if I can simply love them and listen. Minding my own beeswax also says something powerful to the person I love: I believe in you.

Is there someone in your life you're trying to fix? How good are you at just listening?

Dear God, remind me that it's not my job to fix those that I love. They have you! Help me stay in my lane.

MAY 8

GO WILD

ALICE THE ELEPHANT

"We spirit animals are the winged, scaly, four-legged envoys of the divine. We can be extremely helpful to you who live in the world of form. We can help you to find your footing and adopt a useful style to accomplish all you came here to do. In exchange, we only require your loving awareness."

SARAH

WHETHER YOU'RE GOING THROUGH A divorce, were just diagnosed with a chronic condition, are trying to write your first book, or are tackling something else challenging, I have one piece of advice (if you're asking): connect with a core beastie, a spirit animal who can help you! My friendship with Alice has helped me find the courage to be myself, to trust life, and to find faith in this unpredictable process we call life. The cost for all those priceless gifts? Only my attention and time.

What wild animal do you admire most, and why?

Dear God, help me forge and deepen my connections to the wild ones so I may find my own unique power and respect the unique powers of others.

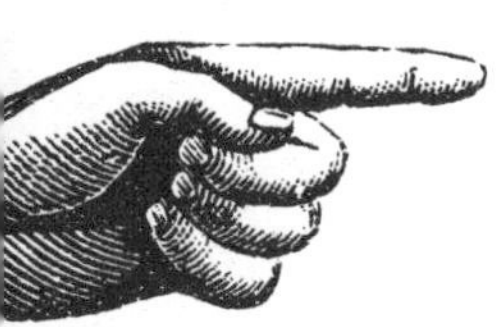

GO TO FOLLOWYOURFEELGOOD.COM/DISCOVER-YOUR-CORE-BEASTIE TO GET ACCESS TO A GUIDED MEDITATION TO FIND YOURS.

STAY OPEN

ALICE THE ELEPHANT

"Relationship is what you are here to master: with yourself and others. A few guidelines will help you when engaging with others. No matter what your ego tells you, respect all beings. Listen to them with an open heart. You are not here to control them, nor should you be subservient to them."

SARAH

My brain can be so overstuffed with preconceived notions about people I have never met, based on appearance alone. My imagination's capacity often astonishes me with such judgments. But when I sit and focus on listening, people usually turn out to be nothing like I'd thought they'd be. I try to remember that no matter how I perceive another being, we are all only children in this realm of the infinite that we call the Universe.

Try listening today with an open heart to someone who challenges you.

Dear God, guide me to foster better relationships with others.

MAY 10

LIVE IN HARMONY

ALICE THE ELEPHANT

"Trees are some of the oldest friends you humans have. This is why you feel such a surprising intimacy with them. Trees are experts when it comes to playing well with others, which is why you should spend as much time with them as you can. Sit beneath a tree for ten minutes and politely ask it to teach you something. You'll see what I mean."

SARAH

I WENT TO GO SIT BENEATH a particular tree and to ask it for a teaching. New to that sort of communication, I felt a bit nervous. But I plunked down beneath the tree and silently asked. Thirty minutes later, I didn't want to leave! I'd learned so much about not only the tree I sat beneath but another neighboring tree, insects, birds, and a whole world of relationships taking place all around. There was so much honoring of individuality going on, and yet the greater good seemed to take precedence. It was so welcoming!

Talk to a tree today for a few minutes. Ask it to teach you something it knows.

Dear God, show me how to live alongside others harmoniously.

USE THE JUICE

ALICE THE ELEPHANT

"Making is prayer. Kneading bagel dough. Dancing a paso doble. Strumming a pixie lute. Illustrating a comic. Curating a wine list. Painting on eyeliner. Collaborating on a tattoo. Don't hoard your best ideas. Use them up, so more can rise. Honor your true Source—the mysterious nothingness that hums and vibrates with everythingness."

SARAH

ALICE ONCE EXPLAINED TO ME that we are like God's most loved paintings. We are living prayers. Have you ever made something you were really, really happy about—a perfect soup, a collage that gave you a zing? Not that it won any awards; just that it pleased you? Alice told me God feels that way about us, his creations! I used to worry that if I used up my favorite ideas about making something, no better ideas would ever come. I have found that what Alice says is true. The more we give away, the more will come.

Make something today!

Dear God, thank you for helping me express my favorite ideas in the best ways possible.

MAY 12

BE A GOOD STEWARD

ALICE THE ELEPHANT

"The best approach to money is to know that it doesn't belong to you. Where do you think it all comes from in the first place? You've been entrusted to use money wisely. So listen. You will always be guided. And when you make mistakes, correct them."

SARAH

I CAN ALWAYS TELL WHEN MY needy shadow self is running the show because it wants to go shopping for things I don't need. The other day, a new bathrobe arrived in the mail after such an episode. In my moment of experiencing an attack of lack and fear, I'd decided I needed to replace my perfectly functional fuzzy bathrobe with a new one. The new robe arrived when I had regained my sanity (at least temporarily) and was living in immense appreciation of life. I joyfully returned it. When I listen carefully, guidance is always there, and when I follow it, every gift I give and every purchase I make brings ever more peace.

When drawn to purchase something, check in with yourself. What guidance do you receive from Source?

Dear God, please remove my craving for more than enough.

HONOR YOURSELF

ALICE THE ELEPHANT

"Food—some days it seems like it's all you think about. It is important to think a bit about it. With experimentation, you can fairly quickly learn which foods nourish you and leave you sustained with vibrant energy and which foods leave you empty and endlessly craving more. Choosing to eat food grown and made with love honors the whole of Creation."

SARAH

THERE CAME A MOMENT IN my life when I realized I was downing bowls of muesli and handfuls of chocolate chips every day in the afternoon, when I wasn't even hungry! I got curious. Eating that way felt really terrible, like going against myself. With observation, I realized that food had become a drug I used to calm my frayed nerves or to dull the experience of strong emotions. Finding my way back to integrity with myself was a journey that radically changed my body, my relationships, and my relationship to spirit.

Eat a meal today that honors your body.

Dear God, teach me what I need to know to honor my body, this beautiful and perfect vehicle you've given me.

MAY 14

LOOK AGAIN

ALICE THE ELEPHANT

"What you would designate a 'failure' is simply a situation where you didn't reach the goal you'd set for yourself. But the Creator / God / the Universe had an entirely different goal for you in mind. When you discover that hidden goal, you'll see that what happened wasn't a failure but an initiation. You were simply being prepared for next-level creating."

SARAH

NAIVELY, PERHAPS, MY GOAL WHEN I published my first book was to sell 10,000 copies. I don't know where that number came from, but it felt like a nice stretch. A savvy person in the industry told me it was extremely unlikely. She was right. I sold more about three thousand copies. I could have considered that a failure, but I acknowledged I was taking a crash course in publishing. A few years later, my first self-published book inspired Sounds True, a wonderful and established publishing company to publish The Book of Beasties, a spirit animal encyclopedia I'm extremely honored to have written and helped design.

What past failure of yours led you eventually to a great success?

Dear God, thank you for each and every lesson you give me.

MAY 15

GET DOWN

ALICE THE ELEPHANT

"How do you pray? I suggest this good, old-fashioned method: get on your knees, say hello, and drop a little (or a lot!) of gratitude, for starters. Share any bafflement you might have. Request help. Always make it clear that you really want to go along with the master plan, whatever it is. Even if you're scared of what that might mean. Ask for the willingness to accept it."

SARAH

I HAVE LEARNED SO MUCH FROM asking Alice and many others about prayer and how to "do it." I used to pray with a lot of specific requests and details. Over the years, it's gotten simpler. I express a lot of gratitude when I pray, and my main requests are: 1) please guide me, 2) remove anything in me that obstructs my ability to be helpful, and 3) thy will be done. That last bit was added more recently. It has taken me longer than the average bear to submit to the idea that I am not in charge. Getting on my knees reminds me I'm here because of the grace of something greater.

Try getting on your knees today (if it's physically possible, of course) and praying. How does it feel?

Dear God, I am open and ready to participate in your master plan. Please help me accept it.

FORGIVE YOURSELF

ALICE THE ELEPHANT

"When you feel none too proud of your actions, don't despair or stand in self-judgment. Forgive yourself. Ironically, it's the humble thing to do. You're as innocent as a child who still has much to learn. Apologize. Ask how you might repair the damage. Then snuggle back up to me and that peace that passeth all understanding."

SARAH

JUST WHEN I THOUGHT I had evolved and finally learned my lesson for good, I did it again. Sleep-deprived, I reacted crankily to my kids for not letting the dogs out when they got home from school. Dang it. That wasn't who I wanted to be. I apologized within a few minutes and began making amends soon after. I also confessed my misstep to my friend Judy and lamented my failure. She told me I had permission to be human.

Where do you need permission to be human?

Dear God, remind me that it's okay for me to make mistakes. Give me the humility and guidance to right my wrongs. Help me stay close to you.

MAY 17

LET IT

ALICE THE ELEPHANT

"One of the things we want you to do is allow all good to flow through you. You can learn how by watching the wind tickle the leaves on an apple tree. There is a relaxed allowing underway in those branches. This is the best approach to life."

SARAH

NATURE! WHAT WOULD I DO without you? You show me everything I need to know—like how to relax. Relaxing and letting things happen sounds so simple, but it's not always easy. At times, when I catch myself barely breathing, shoulders nervously drawn to my earlobes, I remember to connect with those pliant branches, that fluttering lightness of the leaves, and suddenly I am breathing again. Not shallow little huffs, but nice, flowing rivers of breath. In that state, I can even handle the dog at the front window going crazy over the mailman. It's all okay.

Try being an apple tree in a breeze for a moment. Can you feel that relaxed lightness?

Dear God, make me a sweet conduit for your peaceful goodness.

MAY 18

HARDLY WORKING

ALICE THE ELEPHANT

"If you follow your divine inner compass, you'll easily find a balance between work and rest. Too much work brings discomfort and a decrease in productivity, which cannot be restored without rest. Too much rest causes discomfort and a pull for you to be of service."

SARAH

WHEN I WAS GROWING UP, our family would sometimes haul shingles up a steep cliff on the weekends. For fun. My dad loved his job as a dermatologist and often did scientific research, just for fun. Maybe that's why leisure hasn't always come naturally to me. I have been curious about my driven nature. Is it sometimes workaholism in disguise? Alice has taught me that I am worthy whether I'm lying on a blanket in the backyard cloud-skrying or writing 2,000 words. I'm grateful for an inner guidance system that tells me when to start and when to quit. Life is better when I listen.

How do you honor your inner guidance system? What does rest look like for you?

Dear God, help me be aware of my inner guidance system so I can practice healthy productivity.

GET IT STARTED

ALICE THE ELEPHANT

"There will be days when you need to gin up your 'Let's get crackin'!' energy. Nobody can do it for you. Once you decide that today is a day of action, we'll be right with you, in lockstep, ready to guide and uplift you every step of the way. Getting to bed early the night before is half the trick."

SARAH

When I left my medical practice, hoping to find a new vocation that would create health in myself and others, a strange thing happened. My workload had always been predetermined by the hospitals and clinics, my mission handed to me every day. For example, "Diagnose and issue formal reports on all of these cases by six p.m. today." Away from the hospital, in my home office, I had to be the boss of me. As my own manager, I learned to find my own excitement for the things I wanted to accomplish. No doctor or patient was waiting on a report from me. Nobody would know or care if I did nothing (except me!). I had to determine what would be most meaningful for me.

If you are the boss of you, what is worth deciding to accomplish?

Dear God, may I take inspired action on projects beneficial for myself and others.

MAY 20

GET UP

ALICE THE ELEPHANT

"If you want to supercharge your days, make a habit of watching the sun rise. Sunrise is, hands down, the most powerful time of day. Witnessing this everyday miracle will bring extraordinary insights. Harmonizing with the sunrise cycle creates harmony in your life."

SARAH

I HAVE A WONDERFUL WALKING BUDDY. Paula and I usually stick to the trails and roads near our homes. One day, we decided to get up a bit earlier and walk on the beach instead. It happened to be one of those extraordinary mornings where a coral and deep violet sky lit up the mirror-like surface of the calm water. Paula looked at me, eyes wide, and said, "And this happens every single day!" We were in total awe. Witnessing the sunrise is always incredible, even when it's obscured by fog, because you realize you've never seen a morning quite like this one.

Would you be willing to make a date with the sunrise this week?

Dear God, thank you for the sun that makes everything here possible.

STAY TRUE

ALICE THE ELEPHANT

"Staying in integrity with yourself means being willing to be uncomfortable. If you want to know peace, you must learn to be honest with yourself and others in everything you do."

SARAH

THE OTHER DAY, I WAS on the phone with a stranger from the internet (don't ask) and overheard myself tell them a little white lie. The "lie" was that I agreed verbally with what they'd said, even though I did not at all agree. Wow. And that was a complete stranger I was trying to people-please. My inner seven-year-old still longs be sure nobody feels hurt by a difference of opinion. But nobody needs that type of kindness. Being honest doesn't mean I have to argue or be critical. Rather than betraying myself, I can allow an awkward silence to exist.

Practice telling the truth in all things today.

Dear God, help me get in and stay in integrity with myself in all of my interactions.

MAY 22

IN GOOD TIME

ALICE THE ELEPHANT

"Never let hurry into your frequency. Time is a strange beast. You'll find that if you relax, all that needs to be done will get done in the time available. Avoiding a pressured pace prevents many problems."

SARAH

MY MOTHER INTRODUCED ME TO the marvelous practice of reading a few pages of a book in the morning after praying. I finally found a book I wanted to do that with. As I began reading it each day, I noticed I didn't feel satisfied after three pages. I wanted to read more. But reading more made me run out of time in the morning for other critical things, like bathing. I realized I'd begun to treat that sacred book like another chore—something I needed to finish. I want to get everything done quickly so I can move on! Move on to what? I have to remind myself that this morning practice of reading three pages is sacred and there is no rush to complete it.

Use this mantra today: "Whatever needs to be done, will get done."

Dear God, help me pace myself and relax.

BEGIN WITH THANKS

ALICE THE ELEPHANT

"Launch every morning with a big, juicy thank you for everything you've been given and things will go better than you can imagine. Be specific. Give thanks for the dollop of fig jam that boosted your cannellini bean salad. Give thanks for your loving mother who never stops praying for you. Give thanks for the new inspiration your child received about what she'd like to be when she grows up. And give thanks for that crick in your neck reminding you to take it easy. Be thankful for all of it."

SARAH

THERE IS NOTHING MORE POWERFUL than gratitude. Thank you. Thank you. Thank you. Many days this is my only prayer.

Share a gratitude attack. Name three things you appreciate right here, right now. Share this gratitude list with another person and ask them to share theirs with you.

Dear God, thank you. Thank you. Thank you.

MAY 24

LOVE NEVER ENDS

ALICE THE ELEPHANT

"Sometimes it can feel as if life is rushing by. The days and weeks fly, leaving you breathless and desperate to slow it all down. When you feel this way, it's more important than ever to love like crazy, forgive, apologize (when necessary), and be grateful. Taking these actions will remind you of the timelessness of your soul."

SARAH

I REMEMBER WHEN OLDER PARENTS WOULD stop me when I was out with my little kids and say, "Oh, childhood just flies by. Enjoy it while it lasts." I didn't really understand what they meant. I was too tired. Now that my kids are in college, the house can get eerily quiet. Out of nowhere, grief jabs at me: "Where did the time go? I wasn't quite done raising them yet." But when I get out of my thoughts (Panic! Time is running out!) and get back into my heart (No, it's not, I'm still here!), I send a flurry of loving and silly GIFs to my kids' phones and remember that loving them is forever.

What loving action could you take when the wistfulness of time hits you?

Dear God, help me let go of my fears and love the heck out of now.

LEAN IN

ALICE THE ELEPHANT

"When things happen that you didn't expect or want to happen, it's tempting to simply react. I heartily encourage you, instead, to imagine how you might respond. How might one of your wise heroes handle such a situation? What would you need in order to step into that type of response? Perfection is never the goal, but making headway is definitely desirable."

SARAH

I HAVE DIFFERENT HEROES FOR DIFFERENT situations. When one of my books gets a scathing review on Amazon and it stings, I head straight for Elizabeth Gilbert on Amazon to read her one-star reviews for Eat Pray Love and remind myself that what others think about my writing is none of my business. When strangers on the internet want to pick a fight and I begin to fantasize clever retorts, I remember Martha Beck's wise words for such situations: "You could be right." And then I move on without commenting back.

Who is one of your heroes—the one who responds skillfully to challenges?

Dear God, when hard things happen, help me respond with grace.

MAY 26

CRYSTAL BALL

ALICE THE ELEPHANT

"Elephants can sense the sound vibration of another herd traveling from hundreds of miles away. They can perceive what other beings can't. You too have a certain sensitivity that can make you aware of what is traveling toward you. Do what you can to welcome the change."

SARAH

I WAS TAUGHT BY A FEW of my shamanic teachers that prophecy is always dubious when it is for the masses, but personal prophecy could be powerful. Of course, the future is always changing, which makes it impossible to pin down. Although I may not know precisely what I'm in for in the months to come, I often have an inkling. Sometimes the inkling is to get ready to be more outward. Other times, it's a call to clear my calendar of unnecessary commitments so I can have more time to just be.

What will the next few months require of you? If you have a sense of that, take a tiny action to get ready for it today.

Dear God, take away my resistance so I can be ready to face the transformation that lies ahead.

MAY 27

AT EASE

ALICE THE ELEPHANT

"Ah, worry, that horrible habit. Cease and desist immediately! This might be the single most powerful change you could make. Have you ever noticed that, despite all your hand wringing, you're still here and you have what you need (if not precisely what you want)?"

SARAH

OH THE THINGS I HAVE sweated throughout the years: plane crashes and car crashes, bad weather causing those first two things on this list, and losing my actual mind (that would be really bad!). But none of them has come to pass. So all my scheming and chest and gut tightness have been a waste. In the meantime, many other unexpected and unpleasant things have happened that I never even dreamed of happening. I am working with Alice on eliminating all unnecessary worrying. The program involves gratitude and prayer.

Your assignment today is to love your circumstances as they are.

Dear God, help me accept all the things.

MAY 28

RIGHT NOW

ALICE THE ELEPHANT

"If a chore is wearing you down, turn it into a presence experiment. Do the inane task— steam the quinoa, issue the soccer team end-of-season email invitations, clean the litter boxes—with awareness maximus (turn off the podcasts and cease multitasking) and see how that feels. I think you'll be delighted with your experience."

SARAH

When I was in India, one of the gurus complained about the many people who came to him wanting to pay him money to do puja (poo-jah). Puja is when a person of the Hindu faith makes an offering to the divine, hoping to gain its favor. He said that many of the people paying him to make an offering on their behalf weren't willing to take responsibility to change their behavior. They just wanted him to fix their circumstances for them. He advised that the more powerful thing to do would be to make your whole life puja, to turn your home and office into a temple, to mindfully and thoughtfully do everything as an offering. That made a lot of sense to me.

What would be a first step in turning your home into a temple?

Dear God, help me make my whole life into an offering to you.

BE THE CHANGE

ALICE THE ELEPHANT

"When you see a need you believe you can fill, trust that feeling. Step forward and don't be afraid. These little callings that originate in your heart are the Creative Source calling you forward to play your part in this amazing story we call life."

SARAH

WE WERE GOING TO THROW a grand-opening party at our office, but as we began to create the invitations, our mojo was off. Something was missing. My friend Suzi had a bright idea: what if we made the party not about us, but about the moms living at the women's shelter? We had recently learned that they needed purses. Women fleeing domestic violence often do so with only the clothes on their backs. On the night of the party, everybody who came brought a beautiful new handbag with them, which we filled with brand new lipsticks and perfume samples from a local department store. It was a beautiful night of connection paired with purpose.

What little need is tugging at your heart to fill?

Dear God, show me how I can fill a need.

MAY 30

BE THAT GLORY

ALICE THE ELEPHANT

"Think of yourself as an official global brand ambassador for the divine. In that role, how would you treat the irritable barista who forgot to leave room for your cream? How would you carry yourself as you walk around town? I don't mean you should try to be a saint—nobody's got time for that, but aim to be a humble carrier of that greatness."

SARAH

I OFTEN GO TO ALICE TO ask her how to be a better human. "Teach me what I need to know?" I'll ask. She always responds with kindness and a fresh and funny perspective.

If you were the fresh face repping "The Divine," how would you conduct yourself?

Dear God, help me remember that I am yours and, as such, I can represent you daily.

CONNECT

ALICE THE ELEPHANT

"Tend your communities thoughtfully. Personalities can cause friction. Whether you're with your book club, your cubicle mates, or the condo neighbors, it's good to keep in mind that you're better together. You have a tendency to want to cut and run when faced with intimacy. Instead, focus on showing up and remaining teachable."

SARAH

When I complained a tiny bit to a friend about somebody else in a group we were both a part of and I confessed they made me want to bail out of the group gatherings entirely, she said, "Many things can get in the way. Don't let them. Keep coming." That teaching was profound for me. Whenever I'm in a group setting, it's not unusual for somebody's personality to trigger me a little (or a lot!). I usually sit up in my chair a little higher when I notice that happening, because I know I've got work to do.

Do certain personalities rub you the wrong way? What do you suppose they are here to teach you about?

Dear God, help me love and accept all beings.

June

JUNE 1

BUILD IT

ALICE THE ELEPHANT

"Your daily spiritual practice of meditation and prayer is building a golden yurt in your chest. Every minute you sit in silence and connect with your Creator adds a shimmering sheaf of gold leaf to its interiors. With time, your heart will become a shrine of peace for others."

SARAH

IT'S SOMETIMES HARD FOR ME to get the gumption to practice something difficult for an intangible result. But... a shrine of peace? Yes! That's what I want to become! Alice knows me well enough to share such a beautiful and motivating vision. I just returned from a three-day Vipassana silent retreat, where we meditated for upwards of six hours a day. All I can say is wow. The days since then have been so incredible. I feel like I left behind 1000 pounds of mental junk. I'm clearer and more confident in my ability to watch my thoughts.

What would you like to become? A palace of peace? A yurt of comfort and joy?

Dear God, help me be willing to cultivate peace in myself so I can share peace with others.

JUNE 2

PUT DOWN YOUR RESENTMENTS

ALICE THE ELEPHANT

"Anger run amok is guaranteed to wreak havoc on your wellbeing. Bring awareness to any resentments you harbor and put them down. Surrender the situation or person or set of circumstances to the Creator to solve. By doing this you can get back to one of your main assignments: learning to love others without reservation."

SARAH

MARK AND I HAD BEEN cranky with each other for days. I'm sure it was due to the usual suspects: money, or how to raise kids. He put on his sleep apnea breathing snorkel and went to bed. Somehow, his noisy apparatus irritated me even more. Thankfully, I slept and had a horrible Charles Dickens Christmas sort of nightmare in which I was shown how my life would go if I continued to resent Mark. I woke with tears in my eyes. I loved the guy sleeping next to me. I could hardly wait for him to wake up so I could apologize. The dream's message was love without reservation or die. When I love with reservation it feels like death.

Who do you want to love without reservation?

Dear God, help me see my responsibility in situations where I'm resentful. Help me get clear so I can love without reservation.

JUNE 3

TEACHER'S PET

ALICE THE ELEPHANT

"One way to look at purpose is to think of yourself as a student and the Universe as your teacher. Certain student habits and attitudes make your success as a student more likely. Your experiences will vary depending on how teachable you allow yourself to be. Showing up fully for class each day nets you a 'gettin' straight As' feeling. And there is a special joy reserved for the student who loves her teacher."

SARAH

I REMEMBER THE MOMENT I BECAME teachable again. After several years of being miserable at work (at the hospital), I attended my second formal shamanic training. After one of the teachings, I began to ask a question, but was practically swatted away by the instructor, who told me to, "Stop asking so many questions and go do your work." In that moment, I remember being surprised at myself. I didn't push back. I didn't feel like a victim (how dare she swat me away!). Instead, I thanked her and went back to doing my work. I wanted so badly to learn what she "knew." I loved my teacher.

Are you teachable? Are there certain circumstances in which you could be more teachable?

Dear God, please remind me to be humble so I can learn the lessons you offer me.

JUNE 4

BE TRANSPARENT

ALICE THE ELEPHANT

"Let your so-called defects shine. This is what makes you so fucking kick-ass! Let others see right through you. Laugh together at those neurotic tendencies. Confess why you kept your darkest secrets quiet in the first place. That fear of flying (literally or metaphorically)? Own it! It's disarming to your fellow humans and invites them to be blissfully authentic right alongside you."

SARAH

WHEN I WAS FIRST DIAGNOSED with ADHD, I was filled with shame. Everything I'd read about the "disorder" made me feel inferior. I hired an ADHD coach, who told me I shouldn't tell my partners at the hospital about it or they could fire me. "What? So, I'm supposed to hide this?" Around that time, Alice appeared on the scene and reminded me that all the ADHD characteristics I had were also a gift. I was on Earth to do a special kind of work. That was such a relief. Everything "wrong" with me was what was right with me. Then I began to talk to others about my ADHD. It felt so freeing not to keep it to myself.

Share your vulnerability with another person. Let them really see you.

Dear God, take away my fear of being who I am with others. Help me live free.

JUNE 5

TOUCH BASE

ALICE THE ELEPHANT

"When you haven't heard from a special somebody in a while, resist the temptation to take it personally. Instead, check on them—as soon as you think of it. When some of you 'go quiet,' it indicates that you're isolating yourself. Your love and care for a friend can reel you (and them!) back to the warm comfort of belonging."

SARAH

I USED TO TAKE IT PERSONALLY when I didn't hear from a friend in a while. There is a beautiful Hemingway quote from A Farewell to Arms: "You are so brave and quiet, I forget you are suffering." For some of us, it's our natural human inclination to isolate ourselves when we are suffering. But when we feel that way, all the power to feel better again can only be found by returning to our people. This is not to say we don't need solitude. But I believe we heal through connection. I've learned to check on my beloveds when they go quiet.

If you are suffering, I challenge you to reach out today rather than isolate.

Dear God, remove from me the temptation to isolate when I'm suffering.

JUNE 6

OPEN UP

ALICE THE ELEPHANT

"When you desperately feel like a situation must change, we invite you to find peace ASAP (without needing the situation to change). You might ask yourself, 'If this situation is the way the loving Creator has chosen to help me wake up, what good might be trying to get through to me?'"

SARAH

MY MANUSCRIPT IS REJECTED. I hit a patch of black ice while driving with five kids in the car and it terrifies me. My friend's partner walks out on her a few years after her house burned to the ground. None of this feels very good to either of us. It's understandable that we wish it wasn't so. But it is so. Curiosity is a powerful tool in times like these. It can shift you from, "Why me?" into the more peaceful freedom of being open to whatever is present: from victim (fear) into a hero on a divine adventure (love). I'm not saying it's easy, but the minute I begin to make that pivot, things immediately begin to feel better.

How might your current most challenging situation help you grow?

Dear God, help me trust that this is a kind Universe and that everything is happening in order to help us grow together.

STEP UP

ALICE THE ELEPHANT

"I see you and your heart is enormous. What is it that you long to create? Ask for my help and take a step toward it today. There is no time to waste! No matter how tiny the step, it is a call to the Creation for what wants to come into being. It will not go unanswered."

SARAH

I CAN GET STUCK WHEN I have big ideas. I'm inspired but frozen and not taking action on anything. Hesitating. I'm worried I'm incapable. Or that I'm misguided. Or that it might even be a bad idea. Alice always reassures me that it's important to move. My earnest action is the grease that gets the beast into motion. Corrections will be made by the cosmos. That's part of the process. Together, we can make things happen that matter.

Do you have a twinkling of a grand idea? How could you take the tiniest step forward on it today (without upsetting your ego or triggering too much fear)?

Dear God, give me the courage to take small actions toward my greatest dreams.

JUNE 8

ALL OF YOU

ALICE THE ELEPHANT

"It's unbearable to be one version of yourself in one place and another version of yourself someplace else. The desire to be fully integrated, to be all of yourself, all of the time is undeniable. How could you express all of you everywhere? That's how the delight will come."

SARAH

DURING MY SABBATICAL FROM MEDICINE, I had a terrible fear: I could either be a life coach and shamanic healer or I could be a pathologist MD, but to try to be both would be dangerous. I believed I had to hide my spiritual / creative / healer side at work at the hospital. When my mentor Martha Beck asked me what image came to mind if it could be safe to be both things at once, I blurted out, "A xylophone!" I was thinking of the kiddie type, with the rainbow colors. That image helped me. All I needed to do was let myself play all the different colors of me.

When you think of being you everywhere you go, what image comes to mind?

Dear God, help me have the courage to bring all of myself everywhere so I can truly be of service.

JUNE 9

TAKE STOCK

ALICE THE ELEPHANT

"Sometimes you get hung up on and linger on your errors. I want you to focus on all the thousands of times you've done it right. And also to notice how each of your so-called 'weaknesses' is also a strength."

SARAH

I WAS ONCE ASKED, AS PART of a spiritual exercise, to catalog my greatest flaws. The list was long: black-and-white thinker, egomaniac, judgmental, impulsive, greedy, perfectionist, anxiety-ridden, selfish, control freak. Worst of all, I realized how much I particularly relished playing God. As I sat with each of those qualities, I also saw how each had helped me at some point in my past to survive or get by. At least I thought they had. I noticed I also possessed the polar opposites. I could be selfless, open-minded, modest, generous, relaxed, and carefree at least some of the time. I'm a human being. It's all good.

What is one of your worst qualities? How is its polar opposite one of your best qualities?

Dear God, whenever one of my worst qualities takes over, help me remember I have permission to be human and help me shift.

JUNE 10

EASY, TIGER

ALICE THE ELEPHANT

"Zeal can be an excellent quality and will help you accomplish great things. Just remember to allow a dose of its polar opposite, slacking-off, to balance it."

SARAH

SOMETIMES MY EXTREME ENTHUSIASM BACKFIRES. I want to accomplish things so much so that I burn myself (and everybody else around me) out. For example, a simple decluttering project could turn into a full day of ripping everything apart, leaving much of the house in shambles for days. Or I begin working on a new book manuscript only to get frustrated that my day one progress seems terribly insubstantial. With this reckless, fanatical approach, I often hit a wall, get overwhelmed, and projects are left unfinished. My comet burns hot and then flickers out. I've learned it's best to have a gentle plan—one that includes a moderate number of working hours coupled with dog walks, lunches out, and occasional naps.

What would it look and feel like for you to go easy on something today?

Dear God, help me remember it's okay to go gently.

LOVE YOUR TROUBLES

ALICE THE ELEPHANT

"Your difficulties are precious opportunities to become even more skilled in feeling good. Seek solutions within yourself and from the counsel of wise ones. How to know if they are wise? They are the ones smiling calmly."

SARAH

As I bent to unload the dishwasher, I was hobbled by excruciating back pain. I had to take to my bed. That same pain had hog-tied me many times. I suspected I must be extremely stressed somehow, but I wasn't sure what about. As I lay in bed, I got quiet and asked Alice, in exasperated distress, "*What is going on with my back? Help!*" Alice smiled calmly and said, "*You're exhausted. Long ago, you learned that when you are in pain or sick, you get to rest. Now you believe that being in pain is the only way to get rest and receive love.*" Because of that lesson, I've become determined to let myself rest and receive love every day.

What has one of your past "troubles" taught you?

Dear God, help me embrace my challenges so I can learn from them.

JUNE 12

GO MYTHICAL

ALICE THE ELEPHANT

"It will help if you can fancy yourself as being aligned with a fictional hero you admire. Preferably one with a sense of humor and panache, such as Captain Jack Sparrow. Engaging with such a character will help you go far in this so-called 'reality' on Earth."

SARAH

THERE ARE SO MANY THINGS I want to do or create that seem impossible and beyond the reach of my capabilities. But when I think of Charlotte from E.B. White's Charlotte's Web, or Moana or Snow White, I can more easily believe that the impossible is possible. It's funny that Alice mentioned Captain Jack Sparrow. Though he seemed intoxicated much of the time, he did avoid fighting whenever possible, and he relied on wit and negotiation rather than force in all his affairs.

Who is one of your most adored fictional heroes? How did they accomplish what they did?

Dear God, thank you for all the amazing heroes you've brought into my world to inspire me.

GOOD DAY

ALICE THE ELEPHANT

"It is good to pause for a few moments at sunrise and at sundown to study the sky. These are sacred gateways, opportunities to give thanks for your life and for what is good, and to honor your process in time on Earth. The powerful beauty contained in these moments can empower you. You could set an alarm to witness both until you attune."

SARAH

DURING THE FIRST TRAVEL RETREAT I co-created with two friends, my friend Susan suddenly shouted, "We have to go!" She was clearly excited. "Where?" I asked, confused. "It's almost sundown. We gotta get to the beach!" she said. There was total chaos for a few minutes as we grabbed our flip flops, locked up the house, and jumped in the car. We raced down the dirt road to reach the beach at Hanalei Bay, where a mellow and attentive crowd had already gathered. The clouds were heavenly. That was one of the most beautiful sunsets I've ever seen. Susan taught me about the holy medicine of sunsets.

Could you swing a few minutes to spend time with the dawn or sunset today? Notice how witnessing it impacts you.

Dear God, thank you for this day.

JUNE 14

DING DING

ALICE THE ELEPHANT

"Keep a running list of people, places, and things that ring your bell, and refer to it often. This curated list of favorites is a special part of why you're here. You get closer to yourself each time you spend time with them."

SARAH

At age forty-two, I didn't know much about what rang my bell anymore. Child-rearing and work had drained the feelgood right out of me. But as I began to look around, I noticed weird things that lit me up inside: chicken coops, certain artists and their work, brightly colored bohemian clothing, old-timey images of animals, and indigenous textiles. I had no idea why I liked those things. I didn't usually wear colorful things. I hadn't seen a wild animal besides a squirrel or a deer in years. As I made room for those things to enter my life, my soul began to gurgle back to life.

What is your list of people, places, and things that ring your bell? Would you be willing to post it where you'll see it often, and add to it? Or make a collage of it to support you?

Dear God, thank you for the gift of all the details that delight me and make me feel more alive. Help me remember them and discover more of them.

PEACE OUT

ALICE THE ELEPHANT

"Some days it can feel as if you're spinning endlessly in a washing machine of chaos. Hang loose. Even a spin cycle has a limit. It will pass. You'll emerge clearer once again. Relaxing as much as you can is the best way to get through. Ahh."

SARAH

If you've ever been nauseous in the dentist's chair or post-operatively and you had a good nurse, you were probably told to relax and take deep breaths in through your nose and let them out through your mouth. That advice is excellent in times when, even if you don't feel like puking, you feel like you're at your limit. Whenever I breathe like that, I access a little of the soft, still, restful place inside, and that is very good.

Take a few deep breaths and exhale every last bit of air out of your carcass. How do you feel?

Dear God, help me remember I can breathe any time to bring calm to myself, no matter what the circumstances.

JUNE 16

MAKE TIME FOR THE INVISIBLE

ALICE THE ELEPHANT

"Cultivating a relationship with Spirit is the single most important thing you can do to help yourself and everybody you love. By spending time in contact with the divine / God / your Higher Power (or whatever name you give the Great Mystery), you'll temporarily be given a reprieve from suffering. With practice, little by little, you'll be able to bring a little bit of that heaven back with you to Earth."

SARAH

IT USED TO BE VERY difficult for me, as a type-A sort of person, to justify any time spent sitting in quiet meditation, or even going on a shamanic drumming journey to visit Alice. I had to hear the message to slow down many times before I fully integrated the idea that meditation, journeying, and prayer are generous gifts I can give myself and others. I used to think being "productive" was more important. I've also realized that making regular contact with the divine makes me a much nicer person to be around.

Spend fifteen minutes today with your Creator / Higher Power / God.

Dear God, today I will make time to sit with you or walk with you in silence. Thank you for the peace you share with me.

TEND WITH CARE

ALICE THE ELEPHANT

"Some of you keep your heart locked away in a box, buried deep. Take it out, dust it off, check it for unnecessary clutter or damage, and tend it. Your heart is your altar and your treasure. Breathe life into it."

SARAH

LOUISE ERDRICH HAS A MOST marvelous poem (that you should definitely look up) called "Advice to Myself," from her collection Original Fire. She basically admonishes us to do what Alice is saying. I can get more interested in whitening my teeth and whittling away at my heel calluses and forget to look inside my heart. Now I try to remove everything between my heart and the world so I can truly feel alive and be of service. My heart needs to be examined regularly for fears, hurts, and resentments, so they can be recycled (back to the earth) or surrendered.

Ask your heart right now what it needs from you? How does it want to be tended or honored?

Dear God, show me how to tend to my heart today.

JUNE 18

GOTTA SERVE SOMEBODY

ALICE THE ELEPHANT

"If self-pity is a bullet train to misery, then humble service is the Concorde flight to feeling good again. Serve somebody. Take your ever-faithful pug on a walk, make nachos for a loved one, or check in on somebody. Find a way to be useful to someone."

SARAH

Sometimes I catch myself feeling sorry for myself. Usually it's because of some story I have in my head about not having choices, or a thought that the situation should be different. The cure is often to stop thinking about myself and instead think about how I can be of service. Sometimes being in service looks like putting myself to bed early (so others don't have to endure being around my severely compromised self).

Which option for feeling better might benefit you today—asking for help or offering help to someone else?

Dear God, help me be aware when I stumble into self-pity, so I can avoid that perilous place.

PROUD POLLYANNA

ALICE THE ELEPHANT

"Never be ashamed to spread good news. There will always be those who feel it's their job to keep you up to date on the terrible things that are happening. Let them have their say, but don't let it keep you from reminding others of the beauty, kindness, and amazement you observe."

SARAH

SO MANY ARE ADDICTED TO focusing on the negative that it can be a challenge to point to the light. Sometimes I worry that being positive isn't okay, or that others will be angry with me if I'm constantly pointing out the wondrous. I never want to bury my head in the sand, and I'm aware of the many sad and tragic things too. But Alice has taught me that we must also fiercely focus on what is right and good in the world. Pollyanna was not a fool (I highly recommend a review of the BBC film edition). She was a very holy sort of helper in her community.

Point out the beauty of the world to somebody today. To yourself, for a start.

Dear God, help me be unafraid to point out the amazingness that is everywhere.

JUNE 20

ALLOW SWEETNESS

ALICE THE ELEPHANT

"Pleasure is a gift. (So is pain, but that's another story.) Find ways to allow ecstasies, large and small, into your life. Tilt your face toward the sun for a few moments. Massage your hands and feet with sniffy lotion. By all means, allow yourself the profound pleasure of orgasmic bliss. Each episode of feelgood makes you a better conductor of all that's holy."

SARAH

SISTER SACRIFICE, MY INNER NUN with nunchucks, feels like it would be good if I was always working hard. In her line of thinking, pleasure is "extra" and unnecessary. Heeding her admonishment is a trap that never fails to deliver me to moodiness and woe. As I allow myself sweet moments and treats, I become more equipped to serve others in my life. Without bliss, I am unable to do great work.

How will you get your dose of ecstasy today?

Dear God, teach me to allow the experience of bliss so I can be a better conduit for your love and compassion.

JUNE 21

SYNC UP

ALICE THE ELEPHANT

"It's advantageous to work with the Earth's frequency. Hire some kids to bury most of you in sand at the beach or close your eyes and imagine yourself sinking deep into the Earth's surface and lingering there for a while. You'll discover that the Earth's vibe is patient, calm, and trusting. There's no rush. Every shift slowly happens with right timing. Work from that feeling."

SARAH

I WAS LEADING A WEEKEND RETREAT and I'd sent the participants into the woods with instructions. I had a bit of time, and realized I could go outside too. I ran out to sit beneath a tree. I asked, "Hello, tree! What do I need to learn?" I had done that many times before, and received many beautiful teachings. That time, the tree only laughed and said, Just rest. I curled up beneath its trunk and had one of the sweetest breaks I'd had in a long time. After an hour, I returned unhurried and unworried to the group.

How would you like to attune to nature's frequency today? What would be easy?

Dear God, show me how to be like the lilies in the field.

JUNE 22

HARKEN

ALICE THE ELEPHANT

"One of the fastest ways to come into meditation is simply to close your eyes and listen. To everything. Of course, elephants, with our sensitive feet and ears are extremely well-versed at listening, but it's a skill you can strengthen with practice. Perceive the sound waves coming from everywhere."

SARAH

I WAS SITTING IN A SPIRITUAL sort of meet-up, in a group circle, when it got very quiet. Nobody was sharing. It got so still that I could hear the room's fluorescent lights buzz and the radiators ping. Then the quiet coalesced into a roar. Suddenly, in my mind's eye, I felt God there in the room with us. I perceived roses blooming everywhere in that silence. The blossoms filled all the available space in the room. If I hadn't been listening so carefully, I bet I would have missed that.

How many different sounds can you pick out as you sit here in silence?

Dear God, please make me into a good listener.

LIFE AS SCHOOL

ALICE THE ELEPHANT

"Pain is only a reminder that work lies ahead. Think of it as feedback from your body or heart to your soul, letting it know something new wants to be born. It's going to take concerted effort to learn this new thing. Be curious about what it might be. Ask the pain, 'How are you here to help me?'"

SARAH

HORRIBLE BACK SPASMS HAVE, IN the past, made me an unhappy prisoner of my bed. I slowly realized that those episodes always preceded a learning of some sort. Often, the message was simple: slow down; you're moving too fast. I've gotten better at catching the pain early. When that first twinge hits, it grabs my attention. What just happened? I inquire within. Or sometimes, more importantly, What was I thinking, right before the twinge arrived? For me, the answer I get is often some variation on the theme of me trying to control the Universe or play God, as I am fond of doing.

The next time you have a pain (physical or emotional), ask it what it needs from you.

Dear God, help me make a connection between my suffering and what I'm supposed to be learning.

JUNE 24

SHELTER NEWNESS

ALICE THE ELEPHANT

"As you work on a creative project, you've got to find a safe place or person to share it with. Maybe you start with your dog or guinea pig. Sharing the creation is critical. It begins to come alive when it ventures into the world outside of you."

SARAH

Anne Lamott has a whole chapter in her masterpiece guide to writing, Bird by Bird, on "Calling Around." She shares that, while writing, she needs to touch base with friends in order to hash out an idea or confirm a detail of a story. Austin Kleon, another writer and artist, also says it's important to share the work, because that's being generous. Sharing your ideas will inspire other creatives! This book, for example, only became a possibility because I shared my #100days project with my community. That felt safe. And I was flabbergasted by how much people liked what I was doing. That encouraged me.

What idea needs sharing so you can bring some life to it?

Dar God, point me to the right audience to share my ideas, dreams, and projects when they are in their infancy.

JUNE 25

MERGE

ALICE THE ELEPHANT

"I encourage you to leave the comfortable confines of your four walls and let the wild air swirl around you. Marinate in the mood of the sky, whatever it may be doing. The less separation from you and the whole, the better."

SARAH

GREAT SHAMANS OF OLD WERE—AND everyday humans of today can be—masterful at shifting energies. One of the ways that shamans do this is by working with the elemental forces. In their training, they learn to become one with the elements and their own helping spirits so that they can bring healing and transformation to their people and communities. We are all able to connect with nature. When I'm writing, I get in trouble if I try to go more than three hours without a nice hunk of forest bathing. It somehow mentally scrubs me clean and fills me up so I can get another hour of work done.

What would it look like for you to stew yourself in the nourishing pot of nature for a bit today? Could you merge with the sky?

Dear God, thank you for all the gifts of earth, air, water, and fire that transform and shift everything.

JUNE 26

MAINTAIN A RECORD

ALICE THE ELEPHANT

Keep notes about all the things that you like about yourself: accomplishments, shiniest moments, best features. Inevitably, you will receive less than complimentary feedback. Burn or ritually release any unhelpful feedback, especially if it gets to you, so that it won't stop you from being all that you are."

SARAH

WHEN YOU'RE OUT THERE DOING your best work and getting your ass kicked, you will receive feedback from time to time that's not exactly glowing. This is how you know you're doing great work. When dealing with critics, it's important to be discerning. My friend, author Katherine North, says you will know criticism is helpful if it makes you want to return to your project (or process) to improve it. Ignore all unconstructive feedback. Refer back to your list of what you like about yourself.

Begin your list of things you like about yourself. Post it prominently so you'll see it daily. Add to it.

Dear God, keep me open to helpful criticism and protect me from trolls.

JUNE 27

ADMIRE OFTEN

ALICE THE ELEPHANT

"Make a habit of encouraging at least one person every day. You all need it and, frankly, encouragement is in short supply on Earth. Fire off a quick text. Tell someone what you admire. Avoid generalizing. Tell them specifically what is so fantastic about them or their work.

SARAH

As a physician in pathology, I usually only got feedback on my work when Risk Management had to get involved or when I was coding / billing something incorrectly. I remember the rare and special times when somebody told me that they appreciated my work. It meant the world to me. My experience in pathology led me to compliment everything more often. If I love a song and I know the artist, I'll give a five-star review or comment on their page. If the latte art heart rocks, I'll tell the barista exactly what I love about it. In the work I do now, I get lots of positive feedback, which is so wonderful. Appreciation is one of the highest vibes there is, so praise others' good work. Do it for you!

Challenge yourself to give specific and detailed compliments today.

Dear God, help me see the awesomeness in people and point it out often.

JUNE 28

ENDLESS SUPPLY

ALICE THE ELEPHANT

"There will always be enough of whatever you need in order to create. Looking back, can't you see it's true? You will always be taken care of. Sometimes, in fact, the very limits you railed against created your greatest opportunities. Can you trust me on this?"

SARAH

SOMETIMES IT FEELS LIKE MONEY is the only thing our society values. Thinking too much about money has definitely been a distraction for me. I've worried I was a failure for not being a "smarter" business person. With Alice's help, I've realized that not everything needs to be monetized. And I've learned that there's often a payout given for good work rendered that is far grander than the greenbacks we deposit into an account.

What would you create if you didn't have to monetize it?

Dear God, help me today to discern the difference between my needs and my wants.

STRIKE A BALANCE

ALICE THE ELEPHANT

"Shoot for a 50:50 ratio of creative consumption to output. Fill your gourd with glorious museum shows, scintillating books, riveting films, and the joyful artwork of your most beloved creatives. And take time to discover new resources. Let all the insights, color, images, and other sensory input percolate. Themes will emerge. Bring them to life in your own creative endeavors."

SARAH

ONE OF THE BEST DISCOVERIES about being a writer was the day I realized I could write off (for taxes) many of my book purchases and an online subscription to Masterclass (where I can learn from Shonda Rhimes, Steve Martin, and other amazing creative humans). Every time I allow myself to immerse myself in the creations of others, it makes my work as a writer, ceremonialist, spiritual guide, and human stronger. I get excited! I feel less alone when I spend time in the realm of (or in the actual company of) other artists. It feels right, as Alice suggests, to return at least as much treasure as I've enjoyed back to the world by creating works of my own in response.

Whose creative work might you want to explore next? What class would be amazing to take?

Dear God, help me bring out my finest creative work.

JUNE 30

DON'T CLEAN MUCH

ALICE THE ELEPHANT

"Cleaning house is best left for when you need a break from creative work; not the other way around."

SARAH

WHEN I CATCH MYSELF CLEANING vigorously, it often indicates I am in The Land of Utter and Complete Rubbish, and actively avoiding something creative that's difficult. I'm scared I won't do it well enough (the creative thing, not the cleaning), and it'll be horrible. Sure, a clean house feels good, but so does the lobby of a Ritz Carlton, and nobody is coming over today. If a clean house is all I pursue, I'm guaranteed to die full of the sweetest and most beautiful ideas never executed. That's not my idea of a good time. So I let the sheets stay on the bed another week.

What could you let go of so you can stay true to your dreams and creativity?

Dear God, I want to die creatively used up. Don't let me get distracted with excessive cleaning and other unhelpful activities.

July

JULY 1

GO ANY WHICH WAY

ALICE THE ELEPHANT

"Remember that there are no wrong turns, so keep reaching, dreaming, and acting on joyful impulses. Just don't try to do everything at once!"

SARAH

SOMETIMES I THINK THE HARDEST thing we healers, artists, and helpers wrestle with is the question of whether we're focusing on the right thing. We have so many different options vying creatively, vocationally, for our attention that we wonder if there's somebody out there who can just tell us what would be ideal for us to pursue. The truth is, only we can advise ourselves about this, because we're the ones who possess the souls that love so much in this world. Don't get stuck in a quagmire. Keep striding. Keep your eyes peeled for good ideas. Then act on the sweetest ones.

If there are truly no wrong turns, where would you like to head next?

Dear God, please show me—through signs, symbols, synchronicities, and angels in real life—the direction to go.

AMBULATE

ALICE THE ELEPHANT

"You creatives, healers, and helpers can tend to have more energy than the average bear. Walk it off. Try doing parkour. Run hard. Dance freely. By allowing your energy to flow, you'll avoid it awkwardly coming out sideways with untoward effects."

SARAH

I WAS AN EXTREMELY ENERGETIC CHILD and drove my mother to the edge with my never-ending desire to do activities and "make things happen." In my study of creative historical figures using the marvelous book How Artists Work, by Mason Currey, I learned that the most successful creatives (who didn't go insane or lose their health) kept their balance by doing things like calisthenics before breakfast, swimming in the river daily, or walking slowly around the park at dusk with friends. The carcass demands its due. When I ignore my body's need to move, I suffer, as do those around me. So I make it a point to move.

How will you get your groove on today with your body?

Dear God, please help me love my body every day in ways it likes.

JULY 3

YOUR WAY

ALICE THE ELEPHANT

"Your creative process can be messy. Bring napkins. Always allow yourself to work in a way that works for you."

SARAH

When I was working long hours at the hospital, I came home one day to our babysitter and our kids. The kitchen was spotless. I kissed the kids and thanked her and she headed home. Next, I began making dinner. Approximately three minutes later, our sitter reentered the kitchen (she had forgotten her sunglasses). She gasped and put her hand over her mouth in shock. I looked around to see what was so jaw-dropping. Then I saw it. In my process of cooking, I had flung almost every kitchen cabinet door open and strewn every countertop with produce, cutting boards, cans, and pots. I had created mayhem in short order. I felt ashamed. Now, years later, I understand that such mayhem is a normal part of my creative process.

How do or can you accept your creative process and allow yourself the freedom to do things your way?

Dear God, help me unapologetically honor my unique creative process.

JULY 4

TELL IT

ALICE THE ELEPHANT

"Share your biggest dreams with other creatives, helpers, and healers who can really hear them. They will goad and encourage you into action. Buoy and embolden them and their dreams in return."

SARAH

IN SHAMANIC CULTURES, IT WAS understood that if you had a dream, whether it was a daydream, a night dream, or some sort of vision, it was important to find someone to share it with, to deepen your understanding of the dream. In some cases, the dream was recognized to be one many others had been having, and a group gathering was called to see what should be done about it. When I have a new dream about creating something (a book, a retreat, or anything new), I try to share it with somebody who will understand it. Those conversations leave me more inspired than ever. There's something about talking with the right people that makes dreams seem more possible.

Who could be your creative confidant for your current dream?

Dear God, give me the confidence to share the tender seed of an idea with somebody who can help it germinate.

JULY 5

LOSE IT

ALICE THE ELEPHANT

"Declutter your lair, your calendar, your life. Let go of what's not working. Unleash the Feng Schwing!"

SARAH

I HAPPEN TO BE SOMEWHAT OF an expert at decluttering (for reference, check out my memoir Swimming with Elephants, in which we leave our 6500-square-foot home and sell half our belongings at a public sale). I owe my expertise to the fact that I was, formerly, a stone-cold professional at buying material goods as an attempt to solve a spiritual problem. Even if you haven't been as misguided as me, there are still things that accumulate in a life that must be shed: old notes; dead branches; broken things, relationships, and commitments; too-tight shoes; and other detritus.

What needs to go so you can really fly?

Dear God, please help me release with grace everything that is not essential.

JULY 6

BE FREE

ALICE THE ELEPHANT

"Stop caring who's noticing, listening, or watching. Do the work for you. Even if it means being a damn fool."

SARAH

WHEN I LEFT MEDICINE TO pursue a different life, one of creativity and spirit, it was very challenging to share anything about what I was discovering. Did I dare speak of spirit animals and how beautiful the world was since I had reconnected with the Earth and all its magic? Would people think I was a complete flake? I spent a lot of time in those days communing with Alice. She always reassured me that I need not worry. Where I was headed, I didn't need my medical diplomas or anybody's approval. It was scary to trust that. But I realized that unless I did, I would go nowhere. I had to risk being, as Rumi says, notorious.

Could you allow yourself to be seen as a fool? What foolishness will you bring into being today?

Dear God, remind my ego that I have nothing to lose when it comes to answering the call of my soul.

JULY 7

GIVE IT UP

ALICE THE ELEPHANT

"Stop giving a rat's patootie whether others understand, accept, or celebrate your creative endeavors. Create daily in your favorite mediums—no matter what."

SARAH

IN THIS INSTAGRAM WORLD WHERE you can get feedback in ten seconds on what others think of the work you share, it can be hard not to be discouraged. Sometimes I share something I believe is precious, but nobody responds. Does that mean it's a bad idea? I used to worry. What really matters, I have to remind myself, is that I like it. I can't control whether others will "get" or enjoy everything I make. I heard that cartoonist Lynda Barry complained to her art instructor that she didn't like her own painting she was currently working on. She wanted throw it out. Her instructor told her, "That is none of your business." I like that idea: I have no right to judge my own creative efforts because they are God-given.

What would change if you let go of what you (and other people) think of your endeavors?

Dear God, help me create without fear.

JULY 8

ONE FOR ALL

ALICE THE ELEPHANT

"Even elephants, as awesome and incredible as they are as individuals, always remember that they are part of a greater herd. The herd must always take precedence over the individual."

SARAH

As one spiritual recovery joke goes, "I don't know about you, but I'm all I think about." Being raised in the United States of 'Merica, it's hard to comprehend that the wellbeing of the whole should take precedence over the sovereignty of the individual. As I've grown older and stopped striving as much, this unity sensibility has become more natural and I think more about the legacy I want to leave. I think about potential future grandchildren not yet in my arms. What will they need? How can I cultivate more beauty and understanding for them so their lives can be more blessed? Thomas Moore, former monk and author, said the only cure for narcissism can be found in connecting with the Earth, where we finally see ourselves as beautiful and a part of all things.

Do a selfless act to benefit the whole today.

Dear God, help me forget myself and act lovingly on your behalf.

JULY 9

SEE GRACE

ALICE THE ELEPHANT

"Examine beauty with your eyes. It buoys you up. Indulge daily in your favorite sources of loveliness."

SARAH

ONE OF MY FAVORITE DOCUMENTARIES of all time is Meet Bill Cunningham, the life story of the humble street-fashion editor for The New York Times. He was a kind and eccentric man who admonished us to "eat with your eyes." He had access to the most elegant couture clothing imaginable, but it was the real people of New York and the unique and colorful ways they put on fresh combinations that really lit him up. He saw roses blooming in the black trash bags creative dressers sported in the urban jungle. He helped me see that beauty is more than what magazines and culture want us to see. This is what great artists do.

How could you indulge in some loveliness for a few minutes? Where do you want to go in your mind's eye?

Dear God, help me see the loveliness that is everywhere and in everything, bursting forth like a rose.

JULY 10

BE POSITIVELY ADDICTED

ALICE THE ELEPHANT

"Find and invent new ways to feel wild and alive (or calm or harmonious) that aren't destructive to your body, mind, spirit, emergency savings, or other living beings."

SARAH

MANY OF US CREATORS, HEALERS, and artists, with our delicate and sensitive natures, have sought ways to numb the pain and overwhelm. We've gotten our hits of dopamine (the feelgood chemical) from stuff that became obsessions or addictions—too much shopping, gambling, eating, drinking, sex, etc. For me, most recently, it was food. From my family, I knew alcohol could be trouble, but nobody warned me that numbing with food could be just as lethal to a life. If you feel like you're addicted, reach out today for help. There are so many other ways to get a dopamine hit that won't leave you with a hangover: walking, making art, connecting with other humans, and much more.

Do you feel in integrity with yourself? Or do you have behaviors that feel self-destructive? If so, who might you reach out to for help?

Dear God, help me find a path to living happy, peaceful, and free.

JULY 11

LOVE IS ALL WE HAVE

ALICE THE ELEPHANT

"Never stop chasing love. Even if the po-po are on your tail."

SARAH

THIS ADVICE IS A BIT extreme, but I think Alice is saying we should never, ever give up on believing that an old wound can be healed or that two warring parties can become friends again or we can have all the love our hearts desire. Reconciliation and higher levels of love are always available. Be willing to keep holding the dream and taking action when it feels right.

Where do you dream of a greater love holding court in your life?

Dear God, open my heart so I may have a greater capacity to both give and receive love.

ESCHEW ENNUI

ALICE THE ELEPHANT

"Don't ever let boredom enter your vocabulary. In such a magnificent fortress as the Universe, there is so much to be explored. Find the part of yourself that trusts and open your heart."

SARAH

WHEN I DETECT WITHIN MYSELF a whiff of boredom, the first cousin of gloominess, it feels like death. Or, at the very least, a stubborn refusal to live. Boredom seems to happen when I feel like I'm not in charge (somebody else is) or I don't like how things are going. I try to catch it quick and refocus my thinking. Breathe, sit tall, smile—not in a fake way, but in a holy shit, I don't want to miss the beauty of this life way. I try to find something to appreciate. This never fails to bring me back to life from the brink of death.

In what circumstances do you get bored? Does boredom feel like death to you too?

Dear God, help me stay awake and find the seed of goodness hidden in every moment and situation.

JULY 13

BE GRACIOUS

ALICE THE ELEPHANT

"In the beginning, you imitate to try to access the frequency of those whose work and lives you admire. Eventually, you find your own way. If you've been imitated, celebrate! Not everyone emits a frequency others admire so much they emulate it. Be generous with them—none of it belongs to you anyway."

SARAH

I REMEMBER THE FIRST TIME SOMEBODY used a phrase I thought I had originated. I was shocked they would so brazenly use it without asking me first. I owned that particular series of words punctuated by a period! When I asked Alice about it, she gave the answer above. When the same thing happened again recently, I had a similar reaction. My ego is not easily slain. Whenever I thought about complaining about it to somebody, I realized it would be a fool's errand. I've got so many ideas raining down on me. I've also imitated thousands of times without asking, and nobody has complained to me.

Have you been gracious when you were imitated?

Dear God, thank you for the beautiful gifts of creativity you give me. Help me hold my creations loosely.

CEASE AND DESIST

ALICE THE ELEPHANT

"Oh dear. If you only knew how deleterious complaining is to your experience. Make a commitment to cease and desist. Find a like-minded partner to support you. You'll realize how much your protests have been sucking the air out of everything. Once you abandon grumbling... whoa. You're in for a real treat."

SARAH

MY HUSBAND MARK AND I have a joke. Whenever one of us complains, we chuckle and say, "You gonna start that 21 days over again?" We're referring to the year we attempted to stop complaining for twenty-one days in a row. We were supposed to re-start the twenty-one days each time we failed. At first, we could never seem to get to day two! The dogs bark, somebody left dirty dishes in the sink, and... and... When I complain, I'm not accepting the circumstances of my life. I'm in a state of resistance. When I realize this, I try to breathe and accept. A solution may or may not arise. But I am open once again.

Try not complaining about anything for one hour. Or for twenty-one days.

Dear God, take away my complaints and help me find gratitude so I may walk in grace.

JULY 15

PLAN AHEAD

ALICE THE ELEPHANT

"Find ways to eagerly anticipate events that lie ahead. Take the time to look for something positive about everything you're headed for. This approach will turn you into good company and your chances of enjoying yourself will be exponentially raised."

SARAH

BEFORE ANY RETREAT OR TRAVEL experience I create, I take time to visit Alice to ask what I most need to know before I head out on the adventure. Often, she will remind me to perform small and simple preparatory tasks. For example, she'll encourage me to greet and make an offering to the land I'll be traveling to and to ask for its help with the work we'll be doing together there. Other times, she'll suggest a shift in my attitude—to trust more, slow down, or be careful to be harmonious and gentle with my words. The instructions are always simple, but they help me get excited and be grateful before I even head to the airport. After that, I can show up as a more present host for others.

How do you take the time to prepare yourself for planned events?

Dear God, prepare me to be a blessing for others.

ALIGN

ALICE THE ELEPHANT

"Whatever you do, do it standing tall or sitting straight. Your spinal column is an elevator that delivers your vitality. You don't want a kink in it!"

SARAH

In my spiritual awakening memoir Swimming with Elephants, I tell the story of my twenty-one day pilgrimage in India. One day during that adventure, when I was in a dark mood, one of my fellow pilgrims paused to correct my posture, saying, "You're too pretty not to stand up straight." I felt beyond irritated by her comment—offended and cooking myself in a Crockpot of grumpalicious juices (all sometimes aspects of difficult spiritual pilgrimages). It wasn't until years later that I could see my friend had been trying, with love, to help me. Posture is not to be ignored.

Try sitting up straighter now. What do you notice on a subtle level?

Dear God, make me aware of my posture so I allow you to flow freely through me.

JULY 17

LET GO

ALICE THE ELEPHANT

"Be good."

SARAH

ET, THE STAR OF STEVEN Spielberg's film of the same name, vocalized this idea as well: "Be good." But what does that mean, exactly? I asked Alice. She responded that we all know in our hearts what it means to be good, but then we live in opposition to the very instructions we're being given from our essential self. An example is when my soul says, Love that person! and my ego goes, But… they hurt me. Alice says being good doesn't mean being perfect. It means intending to do the very best you know how. My ego may squawk as I look at a messy room, wanting to blame a certain other occupant. My essential self says to let it go. Being good involves a lot of letting go.

What does your very own soul tell you it's important to do today?

Dear God, help me let go of what I need to let go of.

MAKE IT HAPPEN

ALICE THE ELEPHANT

"You're not going to be a wait around for somebody else to make it happen type of person. Don't and hem and haw. When you feel a desire or see something that needs to be done, muster the courage, pick up the horn, reserve the circus tent, or order the baba ganoush. The opportunity is auspicious."

SARAH

ALICE IS DEFINITELY MY GREATEST cheerleader. I've learned that whenever I go to her with new ideas, she isn't very interested in hearing my reasons for believing things might not work. She favors mindful action. Fearless action. It's as if she can't wait for me to book the tickets and say yes, because then she and a whole host of other amazing and invisible forces can begin to work their magic. In the process, I get to learn a lot about myself and the power of love.

Is there something you're being called to take action on? Could you say yes now to making it happen?

Dear God, remove any unhelpful hesitation from me so I may be fully alive.

CHANGE YOURSELF

ALICE THE ELEPHANT

"When you discover you're desperate for somebody else to change their ways, take swift action. Point your beak in a different direction and launch your self-improvement campaign immediately. What's it going to take to get you into shape? You are the only one you can change."

SARAH

I ONCE GOT SO OBSESSED WITH somebody I cared about. My desire to change them made me miserable. It was all I could think about and it was starting to make me feel a little dead inside. It felt awful to resent somebody I loved so much. Nothing changed until the day I decided to abandon working on them and began to change myself. Through a series of steps I took with a supportive mentor and a group, I learned how many ways I had been wrong. Lo and behold, within a few short months, my resentment for that person melted away and my love bloomed again. My whole life started working better.

Who do you harbor a resentment against? What part of this problem stems from you?

Dear God, help me be aware of the ways I've harmed others. Help me offer loving acceptance instead.

NIRVANA IS HERE

ALICE THE ELEPHANT

"Don't wait for heaven. Look for angels everywhere—the driver of the Tesla who let you in on the 401, the grocery bagger who ever-so-gently cared for your kale, your kundalini yoga teacher who always brings the best kriyas. Bless them and be blessed."

SARAH

When I put on my Mr. Rogers glasses, I'm always astonished. Helpers are everywhere! Why didn't I see them earlier? Look! Look! Look! They're here. They're there. They're everywhere.

Count the helpers you encountered yesterday. Dead ancestors count. Spirit animals count.

Dear God, wake me so I see the grace-filled beings at every turn in my path.

JULY 21

OPEN TO IT

ALICE THE ELEPHANT

"If someone irritates you, I encourage you to get curious real fast. They hold a key to unlock a lesson you desperately need. Something in them is reflecting something in you. What could it be?"

SARAH

THERE WAS A DENTAL HYGIENIST who was so cheerful... and she irritated me. How could anybody be so happy? I even called the dentists' office to be sure I never had her again. Hrmph. One day, I was an hour late and they worked me in, but (of course... surprise!) it meant having her! So I got curious rather than being horrible. It turned out (duh!) she was just a kind person. I realized that in my previous encounters with her, I'd pressured myself to be bubbly back, when I didn't feel good. I can give myself permission to be neutral. Not bubbly or crabby. I can just be.

Who was the last person to irritate you? What might they have been reflecting back to you?

Dear God, help me see the truth in all things.

STOP IT

ALICE THE ELEPHANT

"I see you thinking and thinking, and thinking some more, about a problem. I want to encourage you not to think so much. Go roller-skating, plant some daffodils, relax with a Bengal tiger (a spirit tiger, of course!). Things have a funny way of working themselves out."

SARAH

MY OBSESSIVE MIND ENDLESSLY WANTS to "figure it out" or "know what to do" or "be in charge." I estimate that 90 percent of the things I think of don't require thinking at all to get resolved. They simply require the passage of time. Perseveration is a downright awful hobby, unless you are perseverating on peonies, "O Magnum Mysterium", or a nice sequoia. I am a work in progress, and I'm learning how to let my thinking fall away. I once took Alice's advice and hung out with a whole group of spirit tigers. We slept in a cozy heap for a while, tails flickering occasionally.

Do you ever make time to stop thinking? What methods work best for you?

Dear God, help me release my unhelpful mental patterns so I may experience peace more often.

JULY 23

IT JUST IS

ALICE THE ELEPHANT

"When you await the news of an outcome, you expect it to be either 'good' or 'bad.' But I want you to know it isn't an either / or. Only time will tell. The important thing to ask yourself is: How will I respond? What would be a powerful response? How good am I willing to let it get?"

SARAH

MOST THINGS LEAVE ME CLIFF-HANGING. Will the outcome be what I want or not? Will the world behave as I wish? For example: elections, contest results, grades, cancer cells, pregnancy tests, volcanic activity, book sales, teenagers. Time and time again, such things have not conformed to my wishes. It wasn't until I began to claim (thanks, Jim Carey!) that everything was happening for me (rather than to me) that my experiences improved. What if I radically accept all of it? Can I be that equanimous? Experiencing love and peacefulness amongst the so-called wreckage of the world is a beautiful aim. It's been keeping me busy for a while now.

No matter what the circumstances, how good are you willing to let it get?

Dear God, help me let go of everything, especially the things not meant for me.

EMULATE

ALICE THE ELEPHANT

"When you come across somebody you deeply admire—a global decoupage phenomenon, an electric sitar genius, a 1970s television darling—think of them as being on your soul team. A sacred, golden thread connects you. Name their most admirable qualities and try to embody those qualities in yourself—kooky spontaneity, child-like innocence, Komodo dragon–like stillness."

SARAH

If I see something in a person I admire, then it's also in me. You spot it, you got it! There was a time when I'd lost belief in my own abilities and was struggling to know how I might be of service to the world. I wasn't an artist or creative—or so I believed. Little by little, I recovered my sense of artistic sovereignty. I learned more about qualities I treasured: salty humor, kindness, beauty, encouragement, and a whimsical, childlike sensibility. I began to create my own body of work to reflect that.

Name three qualities of a person you deeply admire. Write them on an index card.

Dear God, help me express my wonderful qualities.

JULY 25

GUARD AGAINST GRUDGES

ALICE THE ELEPHANT

"You can be some of the most generous souls on the planet. However, beware of your resentments. They will literally incapacitate you. Each resentment should be thoroughly investigated and may point to where you've betrayed yourself. Look for where you (not they) went astray."

SARAH

When I first started to offer spiritual services to others, Alice suggested I ask clients to bring a gift in exchange for the healing ceremonies I provided. That was wonderful at first. I received fresh loaves of bread, a yellow lupine for my garden, beautiful agates. After several months, the shelf in the hall closet was overflowing with beautiful things people had gifted me, but that I could not possibly use. I felt irritated by those things. It was time for me to visit Alice again. She counseled me that it was time to ask for money instead (for those who had the ability to pay). After making that switch, I felt great again.

In your most recent resentment, how did you neglect yourself?

Dear God, help me look honestly for my part in each misunderstanding so I can find freedom.

JULY 26

JONES WISER

ALICE THE ELEPHANT

"Be positively addicted to novelty that nourishes. Explore rarely read Sufi poetry. Discover new-fangled kamut and veggie combinations. Listen to a strange-sounding podcast your Alexa suggests. Reinvent, upgrade, and expand daily. Avoid dabbling in dangerous addictions or get thee to an AA meeting or similar. A solution is out there, dear humans."

SARAH

MY BRAIN CONSTANTLY CRAVES NEWNESS. I suppose it's the ADHD gene, the one that's always seeking a dopaminergic hit. I can get a high from shopping online at Anthropologie, eating a bowl of sugar-laden granola, or drinking a glass of red wine. The only trouble is that those three activities, for me, don't provide a lasting feelgood. So I've learned to seek my dopamine hits from more sustaining sources: calling a new friend I've just met, hiking a brand new section of a wild trail, or reading a new poet. Those three activities never fail to soothe me, and never give me a hangover.

Where do you go for your hit of daily dopamine? Is that source a healthy one for you?

Dear God, help me be woke to myself and use only good-for-me sources of joy and pleasure.

JULY 27

THE GURU IS YOU

ALICE THE ELEPHANT

"If it feels right in your bones, no matter who you think might question your choice—your mother, that lady in the PTA, or your Lhasa Apso (Mr. Reese's Puppycups)—you must trust it. Good outcomes are never guaranteed. Your results are your feedback. Remember, life is the school and your teacher is inside you."

SARAH

WE HAD JUST REMODELED OUR kitchen, to the tune of 350 thousand dollars, in the city of Duluth, Minnesota, where nobody in their right mind would do that. We put our house on the market a few months later. Some people thought we were nuts. Why would we do remodel and then sell in order to downsize? We were both doctors! Did I have a gambling problem? Sometimes, choices we make from the soul look absolutely insane to other people. Our choices may also trigger others. Integrity is having the courage to follow your inner nudging, even when it leads to more challenges.

When was the last time you listened to your soul's advice instead of the opinions of others?

Dear God, help me clearly hear the voice of my soul. Give me the courage to follow it.

RISK-FREE

ALICE THE ELEPHANT

"Take yourself lightly in all matters. There is literally nothing to lose."

SARAH

When I begin to fancy myself as being "sure about this one thing" or I catch myself wanting to tell a self-righteous tale about what somebody else said that was "ridiculous," I've found myself, once again, on the express boat to Playing God, my favorite island. There is nobody there to sunbathe with or sip coconut water with. There's only me and my irritable and terribly ill-humored ego. When the sun gets too unbearable out there, I sheepishly take the skiff back to the sweet beach of Humility, where the coolers are full and everybody is making a sandcastle together. It's never far away.

Where could you stand to lighten up a bit?

Dear God, when I drift into your domain, bring me gently back to the sweet beach of belonging.

JULY 29

SAY HELLO

ALICE THE ELEPHANT

"Converse with your heart. It's an often-neglected part of you. It has simple needs. Tend to them."

SARAH

When I check in with my heart, as Alice suggests, it mostly wants to love and be loved. I notice that, after connecting, I tend to be more conscious of my heart. I'll leave my house offering love more easily and being more open to letting love in when it's offered. My heart is rarely complicated, but it is in need of my attention.

Put your hand on your heart now and ask what your heart needs today.

Dear God, help me befriend my heart.

JULY 30

TRUST

ALICE THE ELEPHANT

"When spirit nudges you to offer fiscal support to another, invest in a beautiful cause, or spend cash on necessary creative supplies, trust that you have the abundance to do so. These inspired expenditures will be provided for from an inexhaustible source."

SARAH

"But wait a minute," you may ask. "How do I know if it's a spirit nudge and not just my thoughts?" You can only learn this by trial and error. Observe your next nudge. Maybe it's to purchase something you love from an artist you adore. Or it's to send a check to your hardworking nephew who's dreaming of recording his first album. Or maybe (like I did), you feel nudged to hire an editor and a designer to help you self-publish a little book of inspiration. Start small. If it doesn't feel dangerous to you, do the experiment. Take notes on how it feels and what happens next. If the results are good, why not keep heeding those nudges, expanding, and yielding to the largesse?

What nudge do you feel drawn to trust and act on today?

Dear God, with you there are no limits. Help me be generous with what I have and remember it's all on loan from you anyway.

JULY 31

GET THERE

ALICE THE ELEPHANT

"Your integrity with yourself is critical if you want to thrive. Are you feeding yourself in the way you'd like to feed yourself? Are you spending your time the way you believe it's important to spend it? Are you in relationships that honor your ideal of what a good relationship is? If not, don't delay your course correction. You don't need to be perfect, but you do need to move the needle."

SARAH

As hard as it is to retreat from family and friends, I find that spending time alone with myself is invaluable for assessing the state of my union with myself. When I'm constantly around others and always in motion, it's more difficult to see and acknowledge where I am not aligned with myself. A nice patch of stillness and contemplation can give me the space to acknowledge what my soul already knows.

Do any of Alice's questions above trigger you to think of something you need help with? Who or what might help you?

Dear God, I want to live harmoniously with my soul's desires. Please move me toward integrity as I do the thing that's not so hard and also not so easy.

August

GET CONFESSIONAL

ALICE THE ELEPHANT

"Practice telling others the truth about the small stuff: confess your profound disinterest in the Super Bowl except for the half-time show, or the fact that you simply can't abide hot yoga (it's too damn hot!). This will make it easier to start copping to the big truths, like your chronic tendency to be critical of others and to be a total control freak."

SARAH

I've learned I'm not much of a sports fan and I'm done trying to feign even mild interest anymore. What a relief to simply be myself. I've discovered that being honest about such things has slowly made it easier to confess my foibles. Confessing my darkness is scarier, but the payoff is also much bigger. I allow myself to introduce my imperfect self. I'm okay with who I am and I'm okay with who you are. Let's hang out.

How free do you feel to be yourself? Who would be safe to confess more of your truth to?

Dear God, please help me be rigorously honest with myself and others.

ALL IS WELL

ALICE THE ELEPHANT

"It's all going to be okay. It's all okay now."

SARAH

I'VE OBSERVED THAT SOME THINGS seem to take longer than they need to. That lovely person is still struggling. We still don't know what his CT scan on Monday is going to show. I haven't done most of the things on my list yet and it's getting late. The weather isn't conducive for the event I'm attending tonight. Global warming is on like Donkey Kong. The dog needs to go for a walk and I may not get to it. Things are a mess and, in some ways, they always will be. I trust Alice on this one.

Is there something you're fretting about? Does Alice's advice feel like something you can work with?

Dear God, bring calm to my heart so I may deliver calm to all I encounter.

AUGUST 3

SEA THAT

ALICE THE ELEPHANT

"Check out the ocean! There are stormy bits; wonderful, steady currents; gnarly, frothy patches; and still points too. You're so alike! And you are both so very magnificent."

SARAH

It's hard to imagine that I'm in any way like the ocean, which seems so immense and a touch terrifying and powerful. But Alice is always reminding me I am of this Earth and not a foreigner here. I am just as wonder-full, in my own way, as the beautiful trees and flowers and waters. I like the idea of being a flowy and shining sea full of glimmering waviness.

When you notice the beauty of the Earth, try finding that in yourself too. How easy is it to accept your own magnificence?

Dear God, thank you for the amazing ocean out there and as me.

AUGUST 4

BE DETERMINED

ALICE THE ELEPHANT

"If nothing else motivates you to meditate, do it for the children, puppies, kitties, and other baby animals. Do it for the next seven generations, for your grandchildren and somebody else's. Do it for your ancestors. Every drop of stillness you add to the ocean of peace helps."

SARAH

I KNOW MEDITATION WILL BENEFIT ME and yet I'm still reluctant sometimes. But if I dedicate my practice to the people of [insert name of place where horrible thing happened] who are reeling in grief today, I find my discipline more easily.

Dedicate ten minutes of meditation today to someone, to some group, or to somewhere.

Dear God, bring me closer to your heart today.

AUGUST 5

INQUIRE WITHIN

ALICE THE ELEPHANT

"When faced with strife, keep good questions handy. One of my all-time favorites is the one I posed to you when you were really struggling: How good are you willing to let it get? I'm also partial to What would Alice do?"

SARAH

DURING MY SABBATICAL FROM MEDICINE, I felt so scared. I wanted to leave medicine to find more meaningful work, but how? We had a mortgage I helped to pay. In desperation, I asked the Universe, If quitting medicine is what I'm supposed to do, please show me how. A few weeks later, Mark got a temporary productivity raise that was nearly the same dollar amount as my part-time salary. That sure seemed like a powerful sign to quit. Right? But I still doubted. Alice guided me to ask, How good are you willing to let it get Sarah? Could I allow myself to trust this as a sign? I decided I had to.

Name a difficulty in your life. How good would you be willing to let that situation get? Watch for signs.

Dear God, I offer up all my limitations to you. Please take them.

CHOP WOOD

ALICE THE ELEPHANT

"When you have a spectacular spiritual experience, treasure it, but don't fall into the trap of being crestfallen when you can't seem to replicate it. That experience was a gift. Leave it at that and be grateful. Go take out the trash and be glad for that too. It's all sacred."

SARAH

After a friend died under tragic circumstances, I experienced one of the most powerful and beautiful periods with a group of dear friends. It lasted a few short weeks. It was as if we all dropped our personal agendas in order to be present for the greater good of the grieving family. It was deeply mysterious. And then it ended. Things went back to being "ordinary." I grieved the loss of that special time of connection and sensitivity. Why can't we relate like that all of the time? I wondered. I finally had to let it go so I could do the grocery shopping. Our fridge was empty.

Is there a spectacular experience you cling to, something you wish would happen again? How did it affect your "ordinary" life afterward?

Dear God, help me celebrate the extraordinary times—and the ordinary ones too.

AUGUST 7

IGNORE THE WEATHER

ALICE THE ELEPHANT

"Notice that during the gloominess and chaos of a thunderstorm, the trees still dance their leaves, the ground joyfully drinks up the fat droplets of rain, and the streams sing louder than usual. Don't let outer circumstances discourage you."

SARAH

NEARLY EVERY SINGLE DAY THERE is something going on that could potentially irritate me: a favorite mug breaks, my hair goes frizzy, jackhammers pummel the asphalt while I try to nap, or somebody doesn't respond to my vulnerable bid for connection. Yet, all the while, if I remember to peek out the window (or, better yet, step outside), I am reminded that Mother Earth is untroubled by my petty concerns. She thrums, soars, reaches, falls apart, hatches, and does so many other things. Indifferent to outcomes, she strides on with her determination to create.

What do you need to ignore today in order to be creative?

Dear God, help me avoid the quagmire of woe-is-me and other distractions so I may be of service to you.

KNOW IT

ALICE THE ELEPHANT

"See through my eyes. Can you see how good your prospects are when you set out to make a difference today? Can you feel the absolute peace from the top of your head to the tips of your toes? Can you palpate your pulsating potential?"

SARAH

TAKING A MOMENT TO WHISPER a prayer, put my feet on the earth, or pick up my drum or rattle and go for a visit to the invisible realms where Alice and the other helping spirits dwell never fails to help me know the truth Alice is pointing at—to take a look around from her perspective.

How could you increase your contact with the divine today?

Dear God, please help me know I'm always connected to you.

HOW GOOD ARE YOU WILLING TO LET IT GET?

AUGUST 9

EXPERIENCE IT ALL

ALICE THE ELEPHANT

"See if you can feel as many feelings as possible today. Tinkle the ivories and ebonies from grief all the way to elation. It's why you're here."

SARAH

FEELING THE HIGHS AND LOWS of life is not easy! Many of us have developed a fairly strong internal governor that stops us from extremes of feeling, like bursting into tears or doubling over with laughter. We may have learned (at home, at school, at work) that our feelings are unacceptable or inappropriate. One safe place to feel these feelings is out in nature. Nature can help you process feelings and lift away any heaviness. The Earth can handle our anger so we don't unconsciously harm another being with it. I recommend using intention to send such feelings into the ground where the Earth can compost them.

When was the last time you cried or expressed anger? How did you feel afterward?

Dear God, teach me to feel the full breadth of my feelings so I can be fully alive.

GET OUT

ALICE THE ELEPHANT

"Make regular and recurring dates with the people who buoy you—a monthly tandoori takeout with a twelve-step focus, a Thursday morning sauna and cold plunge at the lake, a Saturday dog park rendezvous with your corgis. These appointments should be protected at all costs."

SARAH

WE ARTISTS, HEALERS, AND HELPERS can have a tendency to isolate. Especially if we're suffering. If you look around, you'll notice that the most productive and successful of us engage in community. They nurture their posse. Solitude is helpful, but loneliness can be deadly.

Grab your phone and text someone to set up a get-together.

Dear God, remind me that, like the honeybees, I won't thrive without good company.

AUGUST 11

OPEN TO OMENS

ALICE THE ELEPHANT

"Don't forget that The Great Mystery can speak to you through absolutely anything or anyone it chooses. Look up at the swaying branches of the trees and down to the ground where hair ties, forgotten pennies, and other objects have gathered. Unexpected beings and objects can provide the insight you so desperately need."

SARAH

YEARS AGO, DESPERATELY NEEDING WISDOM, I stumbled onto the idea of totems and omens. Though it sounded somewhat dubious, I began to pay close attention to the animals that crossed my path. My awareness began to expand. When I inquired, the beasties showed up and provided powerful insights and answers to questions I was previously unable to answer. That all happened because I began to open up to the possibility that everything that exists is alive and filled with spirit.

Open your eyes today and explore with the question What do I need to learn today? Notice what and who shows up.

Dear God, help me pay attention to important details so I perceive what I most need to know.

AUGUST 12

GO ALL THE WAY

ALICE THE ELEPHANT

"When you rest, slack off 100 percent. When you're sick, allow yourself to really be ill. When you paint, paint wholeheartedly. This may sound simple, but I assure you that you can improve here, sailor!"

SARAH

ONE WINTER, I FOUND MY husband Mark in the bedroom, fully prostate from the flu. He seemed to be doing something different than he normally did when he was sick. "Are you okay?" I asked. "Oh, yeah. I'm good. I'm just really going with this sickness thing. I'm leaning in." I had never considered the idea of fully inhabiting an unpleasant condition. I knew I should be fully present with my kids, my writing, and maybe cooking dinner. But why would I want to go all Eckhart Tolle in the present moment if I felt like crap? Mark assured me it was a totally awesome experience.

Try being fully present with an unpleasant experience and notice what happens.

Dear God, please help me fully embrace my reality, no matter what.

AUGUST 13

WITH GRACE

ALICE THE ELEPHANT

"When you're scared to do the thing you know you're destined to do, I suggest—of course!—that you do it. But do it from the place where you are held in the palm of God's hand. This will make it so much easier."

SARAH

CEREMONY IS ONE OF MY favorite things to experience in the world. Gathering with others in sacredness for prayer and transformation is one of the reasons I believe I'm here. But when I'm in charge of a ceremony, I can get so stressed about it. My fretting and angst is always a signal that my ego is in charge and thinks it has to do things perfectly or to make everybody happy and meet all their expectations. When I remember it's not about me (duh! it's about The Great Mystery!), I can catch my breath and exchange frantic mental scrambling for calm preparation. Putting myself and the whole shebang in God's hands helps.

How could you do that hard thing you know you're supposed to do from a place of grace?

Dear God, I place all my worries and perfectionism in your hands. They're too much for me to handle. Thank you.

PRAYER ISN'T FOR GOD

ALICE THE ELEPHANT

Sarah: "What's the point of praying for the highest good of all or praying for God's will to be carried out? Isn't God's will a given, Alice?" *Alice: Praying isn't for God, silly. The benefit is for you. When you pray, you feel better. And when you feel better, you do better."*

SARAH

I USED TO WORRY A LOT about how to pray. Was it okay to pray for strangers? What if they didn't want my prayers? What about prayers with specific request for good grades, truckloads of money, or the perfect job? Lately, I've landed on a more humble sort of prayer: thy will be done. I pray for that great power to take care of all of it. It's such a relief. And I feel better every time.

What do you ask for when you pray?

Dear God, I place my life in your hands. Your will be done. Give me the courage to carry out my part in your plan.

AUGUST 15

WHAT COULD IT BE?

ALICE THE ELEPHANT

"When things don't go your way, the first impulse can be frustration. You cry, 'Why isn't this going well?' But you're forgetting there's something brilliant is behind all this. The Great Mystery. Remaining curious is the best defense against disappointment."

SARAH

I TRAVELED IN A VERY LONG and very expensive Uber ride, to get to my book signing that only two people attended. That might have looked like a terrible waste of gas and time, but Alice directed me to focus instead on those two people. Why had they come? I made two great connections that day with fellow animal-lovers and healers. Years ago, I created an amazing retreat for humans to commune with whales in Baja under the full moon. Not one person signed up. I was baffled. Was it me? We had to cancel the whole trip. Then, when the dates rolled around when I should have been in Baja, one of my kids needed me to be there for them.

What recently disappointed you? Do you have any clue why it happened that way? Was there a lesson?

Dear God, I surrender fully to your plan. Help me keep my mind open.

HOLD ON LOOSELY

ALICE THE ELEPHANT

"Everything happening here on Earth is to be held rather lightly. It's not that it's not important, but neither is it as deadly serious as so many of you make it. Lighten up, Francis!"

SARAH

MY BRAIN CAN REALLY GET hooked on some topics. "This blizzard [or other intense weather pattern] is terrible! People could die!" Or "I can't believe that government official is treating people in such an inhuman way!" All this and more can happen in a span of five minutes as I commute to my office. The truth is that the blizzard is happening and the official is in charge at the moment, whether I like it or not. It won't last forever. Nothing does. I try to remember to breathe and let it go. It all passes.

What would lightening up look like for you? What or who do you need to take less seriously?

Dear God, please take this heaviness from my heart and my mind so I may lighten up.

AUGUST 17

BE TEACHABLE

ALICE THE ELEPHANT

"Sometimes, your biggest obstacle is your desire to be perfect, or to be superb at everything you do. I want to remind you: that's not why you are here. You're here to learn. The greatest students are not flawless. They are open and willing to grow."

SARAH

I HAVE NEVER IN A MILLION years thought of myself as a perfectionist. I thought perfectionist people were like Martha Stewart. Perfectionists were perfectly coiffed and had their nails done every week. They color-coded their canned goods. My perfectionism was much sneakier. I was really hard on myself when I made a typo. I felt ashamed if I didn't get a standing ovation when I gave a speech. I beat myself up for not being able to "do it all" at work and at home. Alice and the spirits of nature have shown me that perfect (at least the way I conceptualized it) does not exist on this planet. I was insulting life itself every time I tried to be flawless.

Where do you need to grant yourself (or others) permission to be human?

Dear God, help me accept myself fully.

LET IT BE

ALICE THE ELEPHANT

"Don't dwell on your mistakes. Pitching your yurt there will lead to moodiness and grief. Let it all be. Let it all go. Step into the possibility of this blazing moment. How much can you expand?"

SARAH

Sometimes, driving around in the car, I'll suddenly say, "Oh geez!" out of the blue to nobody in particular. One of the kids will say, "What? What is it?" What happens is that I'm replaying a conversation where I said something cringe-worthy or I'm remembering the time a client called me from the front porch of my office when I'd forgotten I her appointment. Horrors! My brain loves to make tiny shame boomerangs that ricochet around in my head. Sheesh. I breathe and let it go... until it happens the next time. Perseveration on what went not so well is never helpful.

How do you do with letting go of mistakes?

Dear God, help me let go of everything that doesn't serve me.

AUGUST 19

LIVE WITH HONOR

ALICE THE ELEPHANT

"Instructions for life under any and all circumstances: sit tall, breathe, pay attention, and be in awe of this greatness."

SARAH

I ONCE HAD A SPIRIT DREAM about the moment of my death. It was not morbid, as you might imagine. There was a glorious (that word hardly does the vision justice) flowering archway with an abundance of climbing roses and other amazing flowers. A huge light beamed down on this glorious entrance. I perceived that in the moment of my death, when I would meet the divine, it would be very important to do so sitting tall with as much respect as I could muster. It would be a profound joy and honor to die like that. Later, I realized that if sitting tall with respect is the best way to die honorably, it's also the best way to live.

Try standing or sitting a bit taller, breathing deeply, and paying attention for a few moments right now.

Dear God, help me show up for my life.

THAT'S AMORE

ALICE THE ELEPHANT

"You are loved. You are loved. You are loved. You can't imagine how much, but try."

SARAH

I HAVE FELT THE ABSOLUTE IMMENSITY of that love Alice speaks of a small handful of times. It was overwhelming in the very best way. I know a little about that kind of love from the magnitude of adoration I have for my children. I am grateful.

If you believed you were completely lovable, what might change?

Dear God, thank you for loving me and believing in me!

POWER LOOKS LIKE NOTHING

ALICE THE ELEPHANT

"Stillness is the single most powerful place you can 'be.' Terrific, orgasmic shudders and spectacular spasms of laughter are beautiful but momentary pleasures. Stillness is the unlimited luxuriousness of peace you can connect to any time of day or night."

SARAH

When I first began to get the message from my helping spirits (including Alice) that meditation would be a good practice for me, meditation felt very hard to do. What is the point of doing nothing? asked my über-productive type-A self? Meditation didn't come easily. Yet, year by year, I've learned that there is a powerful payoff. It doesn't look like much is happening when I'm meditating, but—somehow—when I'm doing it, everything is happening.

What do you believe about stillness? Do you value it? Do your actions reflect that you value stillness?

Dear God, show me how to be still today, so I can ground in my truest power.

NOT SO LONELY ISLAND

ALICE THE ELEPHANT

"When you're having difficulty with a relationship you'd like to improve, imagine the two of you stranded on a desert island. You'd be utterly reliant on each other for companionship and survival. It would be a good idea to be polite, at least, or things might get unbearably lonely. And, who knows? If they found buried treasure, maybe they'd share."

SARAH

When I received that message from Alice, I immediately thought of a usual suspect: my beloved teenaged children. They aren't currently the most amicable company all the time, and why should they be? I'm not. They have the daunting task of leaving the nest, separating themselves from all the safety they've ever known, and being challenged to "grow up and figure it out." Alice's desert island scenario reminds me to approach them gently and with kindness, even if they're giving me the stink-eye.

When you think of a difficult relationship, who pops into your head first? How could you soften towards them?

Dear God, please remove the barriers within me that keep me from finding ease in this relationship.

AUGUST 23

NEVER GO IT ALONE

ALICE THE ELEPHANT

"Just like the Universe, you are expanding. You can head off in any direction you choose. I recommend taking along good company. It will make all the difference."

SARAH

WHERE DO I WANT TO go? and Who would be fun to take along with me? are questions I love to ask myself when I'm thinking of creating a new pachydermal pilgrimage, transformational Ayurvedic dinner party, or co-writing a ukulele power soul ballad. There is a power in two or three that is not there when I am alone. There are also the added benefits of shared glory and shared responsibility.

Who would you love to have alongside you as you expand? What joint venture sounds most delightful?

Dear God, point me toward expansion and show me who would make the journey sweeter so I can invite them too.

HUMDIGGITY

ALICE THE ELEPHANT

"You may have been taught that God is somewhere 'out there,' or maybe that meeting with God is a destination for some future date, like the day you die. I'm telling you, God has never been separate from you. Ever. If you pause and listen, you just might be able to hear God humming."

SARAH

MORE AND MORE I HAVE been realizing that what Alice says above is true. The sense that the divine is "out there" is a suffering thought, when all I want is to be close. I sometimes have to remind myself that this is a problem of perception. God is right here. I can drop to my knees at any time and whisper, Please help! Use me! Show me how to be!

When you pause and listen, do you feel a divine presence? If not here, when or where have you felt it before?

Dear God, let's be together today and for always. Remove my perception that I am separate from you.

AUGUST 25

MOVE THE NEEDLE

ALICE THE ELEPHANT

"Work toward becoming a person you admire. You have what it takes. You simply need some practice. Kindness, calmness, diligence, consistency are all at your fingertips. Try them on for size."

SARAH

Sometimes I get broody when I witness another person who is being incredibly kind or disciplined or talented. Momentarily, I forget that I too can bring my A game to life. I am not exactly like someone else, but if I like how they're being kind, I can bring that quality out in my own life. It feels so much better to see those I admire as teachers and to express similar ways of being, rather than use them as evidence that I'm not there yet. I too am capable of being creative, innovative, kind, and thoughtful.

Who have you really admired this week? What quality do they have that's so striking? How could you bring that quality forward today in your actions?

Dear God, please help me be the best version of myself I can muster on this day.

LEAVE IT AS IT IS

ALICE THE ELEPHANT

"For today, just let it all be. That absolutely gigantic cobweb in the window. The unfinished business with your mother. The raspberry jam that dried onto the kitchen floor in a glossy, sticky blob. Let it all go."

SARAH

MY MIND CAN GET SO caught up in all the things I want to do, should do, or must do. I forget that the most critical thing I can do to change things is just breathe and take down the wall standing between myself and God.

What do you need to ignore, let go, or accept to find peace in this moment?

Dear God, please release the grip on my mind of everything that keeps me from being closer to you.

AUGUST 27

COME ON IN

ALICE THE ELEPHANT

"Put a welcome mat out daily for the divine. Make a request that you be shown what you need to know through omens: helpful beasties who remind you how to be, song angels delivering lyrics to direct you, friendly gas station cashiers who say things that help it all make more sense."

SARAH

THERE IS ALWAYS HELP EVERYWHERE, but sometimes I forget. I forget a lot, actually. All it takes is a tiny shift on my part to open up for guidance. For me, this is often a parking lot pivot. Last week, before I entered the post office, I somehow remembered that the Lakeside neighborhood US Postal Service office is a holy temple. My morning errand suddenly shifted into a sweet and, dare I say, ecstatic encounter with the divine. Postal workers can be diviners too.

How could you signal the loving Universe that today you are open to receiving omens?

Dear God, open my eyes and prick up my ears so I might notice the amazing ways you're always trying to help me.

HEAR THE MESSAGE

ALICE THE ELEPHANT

"Take a moment to imagine you're lying on the earth on your side upon a soft bed of emerald green moss. The sun warms you and you have your ear to the ground. Mother Earth embraces you in her deep green apron of wonder. You sense her energy and spirit. She whispers something into your ear. What does she say?"

SARAH

When I put my ear down onto the earth today, Mother Earth told me, "It's okay to go slow." The answer to 99 percent of my problems is an earthbound reset. When my thoughts have become dominant, I desperately need to return to my heart and to remember that I am of this Earth.

When you lie on the great bosom of Earth, what does Earth whisper to you?

Dear God, help me attune to the frequency of the earth so I can be in harmony with myself.

AUGUST 29

SET IT DOWN

ALICE THE ELEPHANT

"When you feel like a hot mess, drop it all. Put everything into my lap. Cease the fretting and start the surrender. I can't do anything for you until you relinquish control."

SARAH

One evening I led a ceremony and, in our sacred sharing afterwards, I thought I caught the slightest whiff of disappointment in one of the participants, like they hadn't experienced what they'd hoped they would. My egoic mind latched onto it firmly. I began to fret about her disappointment. Had I done the ceremony poorly? Maybe I shouldn't run ceremonies ever again. The next day, full of angst about this, I was horrible company to everybody, including myself. Finally, I gave it over to Alice. She reminded that I had done nothing wrong, that I don't have to make everybody happy (I'm not tequila). The experience of disappointment may be the teaching for someone in a ceremony too. Everything is.

Is there something or someone you'd like to hand over to whomever you pray to?

Dear God, please take this difficult thing from me. Thy will be done.

EVERYTHING IS PERFECT

ALICE THE ELEPHANT

"Trust the timing of absolutely everything. Remember that it is not you who's in charge. Something greater and more mysterious is supervising the unfolding."

SARAH

I HAD INVITED TWO FRIENDS TO practice a shamanic death and dying rite with me one evening. I was preparing to guide a larger group and wanted to practice. My friend texted me to say she'd fainted earlier in the week and the doctors had found something worrisome with her heart conduction system. She was scheduled for a cardiac test in the morning. Suddenly, I panicked. Would doing a death rite be too much for my friend who was in the middle of a real-life health scare? But she didn't want to cancel. So we practiced the death rite and did healing work afterwards for her with our drums. I realized the timing was more than perfect: it felt divinely designed.

Is there something that doesn't seem to be happening fast enough, or something you believe is happening at the worst time? How would things shift if you simply trusted that the timing is perfect?

Dear God, take away my argument with your timing and help me trust you.

AUGUST 31

ME FIRST

ALICE THE ELEPHANT

"If you long to be a helper, you must prioritize our relationship. Put me first, always. Before breakfast. Everything else will ripple out from there."

SARAH

Insanity is when I expect to be useful to my kids, husband, and parents when I haven't first done my daily prayers and meditation. How could I be so ridiculous? I offer myself permission to be human. I am learning to tend first to that most precious relationship.

How do you prioritize? Does God always come before breakfast?

Dear God, I want to be a helper and put you first. Please remove any blocks within me.

September

SEPTEMBER 1

LOVE WITHOUT WORDS

ALICE THE ELEPHANT

"Touch, a skill elephants possess with considerable chops, is one of the more important tools you can develop. Of course, you must ask permission first. But, once you have it, let your hands become instruments of tenderness. A massage, a caress, or simply resting your hand warmly on another's shoulder fosters connection, safety, and belonging without saying a word."

SARAH

ONE OF MY DEAREST SHAMANIC teachers is a master of the sacred touch Alice speaks of. During a healing with this shamanic teacher, I always feel as though I'm the most precious being that ever existed on the planet. She lets her students know this, wordlessly, with her tender touches. Being mostly Norwegian as I am, descended from people not known for their affectionate nature, I'm working to more deeply develop this powerful tool of sacred touch.

Who could you practice your tender touches on today?

Dear God, remove any awkwardness or lack of confidence from my ability to bring comfort to another with my gentle touch.

SEPTEMBER 2

BE READY

ALICE THE ELEPHANT

"Keep an apology poised on your lips. The instant you know you've caused suffering (and you will!), say, "I'm sorry." Then move as quickly as you can to set things right. If you're feeling fierce, you can even apologize for the hurts that others have caused."

SARAH

When I first took my sabbatical from medicine, I poured my heart out to a coach about something painful that had happened to me. She listened carefully and then did something powerful. She made a formal apology to me on behalf of all of the people in a particular group who I believed had wronged me. Now, that coach didn't know me at all. And, apparently, she didn't need to critically assess whether my complaint about that group was legit. Her apology brought tears to my eyes: somebody believed me. I no longer felt stuck in victimhood. I felt understood and known for the first time in a long time.

How easily does "I'm sorry" come to you? What about making amends—taking an action to make things right?

Dear God, please help me see when I've misstepped, and help me quickly correct my actions.

SEPTEMBER 3

POLLINATE

ALICE THE ELEPHANT

"Use your superpowers to assist, promote, and support other artists, healers, and helpers of all kinds. These modern day medicine people are restoring our Universe. Trust that there is no competition and there is more than enough abundance to go around."

SARAH

WHEN I MEET SOMEONE WHOSE work I love, my heart surges and I immediately want to support them somehow. Then my curmudgeonly / miserly / fear-based self will counter, "But, Sarah, can you really afford to purchase that art?" or "People might get sick of all your posts about other people's poetry, paintings, and books," or some other such nonsense. Whenever I ask Alice about this, she reminds me it's always a good idea to support others in whatever way I feel called. One such urge led me to hire a beloved artist to cover our ceiling in dancing paper peonies. "Wasn't it outrageous?" my miserly ego argued. "No," replied Alice.

Honor any nudges you get this week to support a fellow artist, healer, or helper.

Dear God, help me trust that there are always enough resources for the important and necessary things.

THIS IS NOT A DUEL

ALICE THE ELEPHANT

"Competition is the hogwash of egoic perception. Beware this illusion, because it will block your riches. Remember that you all share one Director, and this Director is only ever joyfully expectant of your very best."

SARAH

MY DELICATE EGO CAN GET tweaked at the slightest provocation. Somebody else's kid gets The President's Award for Most Brilliant Teen of the Millennium, a fellow author's shamanic mystery is shortlisted for the Pulitzer, or a high school classmate's 1 guinea pig photography is this month's National Geographic's cover story. My brain immediately goes to work, asking me why I haven't been successful like that ("Sarah, seriously. You need to get your act together!"). I have to gently remind this demanding part of me that we are doing just fine. Then I go back to cavorting with the divine perfection that relentlessly parades before me.

Has anyone else's success triggered you into feeling like a useless lump? Could you find the part of yourself that could be deep down happy for them?

Dear God, help me celebrate the beautiful accomplishments of others without discounting my own life's contributions, whatever they may be at the moment.

SEPTEMBER 5

GIVE ANONYMOUSLY

ALICE THE ELEPHANT

"Do one tiny thing today without needing to take credit for it. It might not seem like much, but if you plant seeds like this regularly, something important might grow in you: a mango tree of humility."

SARAH

MY EGO GOES ZING WHEN I receive an email thanking me for my generosity, like when someone says they saw my name on the donor wall at the local mental health facility. It's nice to be noticed for helping create something wonderful. At age ten, my sister Maria put her entire savings into the offering plate at church one Sunday morning. She was disappointed when nobody seemed to notice. She'd wanted everybody to witness her great act of absolute selflessness. Maria and I joke that we need a "Give-cam"—a custom Go-Pro camera we wear on our heads to share live footage of ourselves doing good things. Laughing about this waters those mango seeds Alice mentions.

Do a good deed today. Pay for coffees for the car behind you at the drive-through. Pick up some trash. Leave a loving message of encouragement on the bathroom mirror.

Dear God, point out the opportunities for me to do good without getting credit.

TAKE IT ALL IN

ALICE THE ELEPHANT

"Pleasure. There are infinite ways to allow the incredible love you're marinating in to flow through you: reveling in the sturdiness of the otter-handled coffee mug you got at the art fair; admiring the rain droplets quivering on the leaves by the driveway; stroking the perfect, velvety muzzle of your mostly well-behaved pug. This is love in all its forms. Drink it in."

SARAH

I REMEMBER ONCE BEING ASKED IN a self-help quiz, "Do you allow yourself to feel exquisite pleasure each day?" At the time, we had many small children and were working too many hours. I think the last time we had experienced sexy-time was three weeks prior. Not only was I exhausted, I was suddenly also aware that I was apparently underperforming in the pleasure department. Since then, things have improved dramatically. I've learned that while intimacy is most definitely a fabulous delight, it's also good to relish all things blissful.

What was the last true, deep pleasure you experienced? Is there pleasure here, right where you are now too?

Dear God, open all the channels inside me so I sense and know the ever-present love all around me. Fill me with it.

SEPTEMBER 7

SAY CHEESE

ALICE THE ELEPHANT

"Smile. Do it for me."

SARAH

A WISE PERUVIAN MEDICINE WOMAN LOOKED at our group of seekers (who would soon return home after an intense and challenging spiritual retreat) and said, "The world out there is a big mess. So, when you get to the airport, sit up straight and smile. Laugh, even!" She wasn't encouraging us to feel our feelings or to consider more deeply the tragic state of the Earth's ecology. She was admonishing us to be "stubbornly glad," as poet Jack Gilbert suggests, in the harshest of times.

Try smiling now. What changes when those corners of your eyes and mouth lift?

Dear God, help me to be dogged in my cheerfulness today.

LEAVE HOME

ALICE THE ELEPHANT

"Get out more. Disrupt your routine by seeing what (and who!) lies outside the confines of your usual haunts. It will help you grow."

SARAH

I'VE LEARNED THAT, DESPITE WHAT my inner rebel sometimes has to say about it, routine is my friend. But I've also noticed that a routine (for example, morning meditation, heading to work, the usual garbanzo bean salad) can become oppressive over time. Going out to watch the sun rise on the beach in lieu of meditation, working from the new local tea shop for the morning, or using black-eyed peas instead of garbanzos in the salad are important. I get ideas, meet new people, entertain fresh perspectives, and, perhaps most importantly, I get a sweet break from myself and all my thinking.

Where could your routines stand a bit of a disruption? Does any part of your life feel stale? How could you bring in a twist?

Dear God, help me keep routines when they're helpful and abandon them when I need to take a fresh look at things.

SEPTEMBER 9

COME CLOSER

ALICE THE ELEPHANT

"This peace, this calm, this infinite awesomeness I offer to you is always here for the taking."

SARAH

WHEN I GET INTO A semi-hysterical lather about the small piles of dirt building up in front of the porch stairs, anxious that I lack skill as a mother, or I find myself a little too obsessed with the latest Soft Surroundings catalog (does anybody actually live permanently moisturized in a state of wonder at an outdoor porch barbeque in a sassy Moroccan kaftan?), I can instantly take myself out of my misery by thinking of Alice or calmly intending to draw closer to my Creator. Quiet instructions usually follow. The dirt piles will be tackled whenever you decide it's time. No mother is perfect. Recycle the catalog, stat, before you order a full-length faux-sheepskin, ostrich-trimmed onesie for yourself.

How do you respond when dirt piles and other triggers appear on your path?

Dear God, remind me that when my life feels like a muddy ditch, the path back to you is only inches away.

WALK THIS WAY

ALICE THE ELEPHANT

"With each step through your living room, around your cubicle, along a neighborhood trail, or around your jail cell, say, 'Thank you!' for something with every footfall. Be thankful for anything you can think of. This will keep you out of a lot of trouble."

SARAH

GRATITUDE IS A MAGIC MEDICINE. It's the most powerful neutralizer of darkness I know.

How could you make a daily habit out of gratitude? Who else could you play a gratitude game with?

Dear God, with every step I take, help me remember all the ways you love and support me.

DIG IN

ALICE THE ELEPHANT

"The main course here on planet Earth is that you're here to love and be loved. Everything else is a relish, and, like a good chutney, can enhance it. But without the foundation of love, even chutney is meaningless."

SARAH

I WAS IN PERU WITH MY husband Mark, praying hard that, somehow, we would have a breakthrough in our relationship. Our friend the shaman brought Mark and I together during our final ceremony. I knew it was then or never. "Mark, could we renew our vows right here?" I asked him. "Sure," he said, not seeming too opposed to the idea. We sat down together on the grass facing the beautiful, sacred mountain. "I just want to love you and be loved by you," I blurted out. He grabbed my hands, smiled, and said, "I want the same thing." We kissed, spent the rest of the afternoon entwined in each other's arms staring at that mountain, and things have been really good since then. Are you giving and receiving love in good quantity? If not, what needs to shift?

Are you giving and receiving love in good quantity? If not, what needs to shift?

Dear God, help me live and breathe this truth: nothing is more important than loving and being loved.

NO SHAME IN YOUR GAME

ALICE THE ELEPHANT

"The worst mistake you can make in life is believing something is entirely your fault. You're giving yourself way too much credit. Yes, you've contributed in some part, and you should own that. But remember that no one person is utterly responsible for any outcome."

SARAH

WHAT A RELIEF TO BE reminded that I'm never the only one to blame for a "bad" outcome or set of circumstances. Like they sing in High School Musical, "We're all in this together." Both glory and responsibility must be shared.

Do you ever replay in your head your life's "mistakes" reel? When you look deeper at one of those situations, where is it true that others also had responsibilities?

Dear God, help me release any shame I harbor so I can live fresh and free from self-blame.

SEPTEMBER 13

NO DOUBT

ALICE THE ELEPHANT

"Self-doubt is no bueno. It's the ultimate and most tragic excuse! Make the honorable and, ultimately, much more interesting choice to believe in yourself."

SARAH

I'VE BEEN PLAGUED AS MUCH as the next person by self-doubt—maybe more. After a while, it became embarrassing to explain my disbelieving position again and again to my loving and compassionate spirits on the team along with Alice. I had to begin honoring them and all their kind advice and start trusting myself.

Where does self-doubt limit you? What would change in that area if you trusted yourself?

Dear God, remove the doubt that limits me so I can do your bidding.

USE LOVE AS A LENS

ALICE THE ELEPHANT

"Science is just a method, an imperfect but useful way of examining the world. It is not the truth. The only truth is love. So don't demand to see the science behind something that's already been validated by your heart."

SARAH

I HEAR SO MANY SPIRITUAL TEACHERS apologizing for being "woo-woo." I don't love that word. It discounts everything mysterious that cannot be "proven" but is known by the heart. In our culture, we have a strong tendency to worship science, especially when it comes to the care and healing of our bodies. We need traditional medicine—no doubt about it. But to ignore our souls and our spirits in any healing environment seems absolutely banana pancakes. If you have an inkling in your heart about what would create more health in you, why not honor that? Even if it's woo-woo. Especially if it is.

Have you ever ignored your heart's voice and followed logic instead? How did it go?

Dear God, no matter how loud the voice of reason shouts, help me trust my inner knowing today.

SEPTEMBER 15

CEASE PLEASING

ALICE THE ELEPHANT

"Realize that not all people can handle your awesomeness in every moment. That's okay. Toss them a loving 'Namaste' and move on (in peace, love, and joy, of course). Take your effervescence elsewhere."

SARAH

I USED TO TAKE OFFENSE WHEN my comedic musings or my highly enthusiastic nature were not appreciated. Or, when I got baffled looks in response to my delightful conversation-starters in the doctors' dining room at the hospital, I shrunk three sizes. For example: "Did you see American Beauty at the theatre? I can so relate to the wife character. Which character did you relate to?" With Alice's aid, I've gotten better at accepting that I am not for everyone. As my sister, comedian Maria Bamford, says, "If you enjoy caustic, barrel-chested, Polynesian one-liners, my show may not be for you!" It's okay to walk out.

Can you accept that you cannot please everyone all the time? Who is the hardest person for you to accept this about?

Dear God, help me detach quickly and lovingly from those who don't get me (yet).

FINISH IT

ALICE THE ELEPHANT

"Perfectionism comes with the territory. When you perceive that a certain je ne sais quoi is missing, it can be mighty frustrating. Your creative work feel may feel like it's eternally falling slightly short of the mark. Find the place where you are deeply satisfied and not compromising, yet where more tiny things could be tweaked, and then move the hell on, or let somebody else do the fussing so you can begin creating something new."

SARAH

AT THE END OF THE process of writing each of my books, I've had a terrible feeling that, somehow, it would all be better if I hadn't agreed to make some of the changes or if I'd had more time or... or... or. My aim is always to make creations as good as they can be, and then let it go. At a certain point, I know in my heart that it's done, not perfect. It will never be perfect.

Where do you struggle with the idea that you have to do it perfectly?

Dear God, remind me that it's not my job to do everything perfectly today. Help me be the best I can be.

SEPTEMBER 17

LOOK

ALICE THE ELEPHANT

"Find something to love about each day, and find it early."

SARAH

ALICE'S POINT ABOUT FINDING SOMETHING to love early in the day is so important for me. When I miss my morning practice of quietude and some brand of spiritual practice, reading, or inquiry, I miss the chance to get my focus on the right place. When I'm seeing clearly, there's always so much to love. The sun rising. Rain tap tap tapping in the gutters. The weird and beautiful way steam forms over the lake. The dogs barking at the squirrels. Bright light pouring into the windows now that the leaves are gone from the trees.

What do you love in your world in this white-hot moment?

Dear God, help me see everything through your eyes.

DO HARD THINGS

ALICE THE ELEPHANT

"Humility must be fostered. Even elephants, as sick and amazing as we are, have to remember that we are part of a larger herd. To keep your ego in check, do things that challenge you. Surfing, yoga, or any new thing that engages your mind and your body is ideal. Surfing off Cayucos, California, is truly ideal. I'm also partial to Hanalei Bay."

SARAH

THE FIRST TIME I TRIED surfing, my friend Susan pushed me into a wave and I rode that six-inch crest for a good 30 yards. Such bliss! After that, it took me hours to catch another wave. It was frustrating. I had to learn that I wasn't in charge. There was a humbleness and patience required of me to join up with those waves and ride them. The price of admission was my surrender and the entirety of my attention. I always feel that same way in yoga classes. I can't do what the instructor can and I have to remind myself that it's okay. I'm there to be challenged.

What activity is a little bit hard for you and humbles you? Do you avoid it?

Dear God, make me willing to try things that challenge my body, mind, and soul so I can grow.

SEPTEMBER 19

EMBRACE YOURSELF

ALICE THE ELEPHANT

"Maybe you've noticed you get tons done on your young adult novel while lodged in a faux-fur beanbag. Perhaps a bed picnic replete with salami helps you launch your connection with your inner Cezanne. Or maybe you're guaranteed at least four incredible podcast episode ideas in one go if you can work at the overcrowded punk rock coffeehouse. Own how you roll best and honor it."

SARAH

TO BE CREATIVELY PRODUCTIVE, THERE have been times when I've had to wear noise-canceling headphones (appropriate for a rifle range) at home, where dogs bark and children yell (or is that only me?). At other times, I've worked creatively in noisy places where I could blast the same song over and over in my ear buds, which weirdly caused words to flow (the song was "1901," by Phoenix, if you must know). Airplanes are almost always good. Above ten thousand feet, I feel clear-headed and energized.

What ingredients, spaces, or situations help you create? Are you okay with that? If any feel a little too Janis Joplinesque, how could you exchange them for something healthier?

Dear God, help me discover the best conditions for myself and to create and honor them.

SEPTEMBER 20

IT'S WORTH IT

ALICE THE ELEPHANT

"Get help polishing big, important projects, so your idea gets seen in the best light."

SARAH

I HAD TO GET OVER MYSELF and hire an editor to help me organize my first book. The idea of paying money for help on a project that had a very strong chance of never paying me back seemed ludicrous. But, without her help, that book would never have been. I'm a visionary and not as strong with fine details. For some of us creatives, healers, and helpers, asking for help can be the hardest thing. Investing money in our own work can be even harder. Great things are never accomplished alone. Get the help you need so you can make your beloved creation the best it can be.

If you could have any help with your creative and healing endeavors, what would it be?

Dear God, remind me that I never have to go it alone. With your help, I can find the help I need.

GET LIT

ALICE THE ELEPHANT

"Find ways to feel wild and alive that aren't destructive to body, mind, pocketbook, or persons. Take yourself on a mini-vision quest for the afternoon in a hidden corner of a local park (backpack loaded with comfy blanket, journal, colored pens, and a tasty snack). Leave an encouraging note with ten dollars at a bus stop. Have naked beach photos taken of yourself and a friend at sunrise and discuss how looking at them makes you feel."

SARAH

SOMETIMES THE VERY BEST IDEAS for coming alive are born of frustration. I used to wonder, for instance, why women did boudoir photography sessions. They reported that it made them feel empowered. I was confused. Lying on a bed wearing a lacy, black thong that straddled my hoo-ha didn't sound empowering? Some kind friends encouraged me to explore empowerment in my own way. Alice prodded me to take some risks and, to my utter surprise, my experience was very, very good.

Is there something others are doing that irritates or confuses you? How might you explore that in your own way?

Dear God, show me how to live fully, truly, and deeply.

NAME-DROP

ALICE THE ELEPHANT

"Labels like too sensitive, too intense, too much, and too loud hurt. Find new ones, like ah-mazing, born to freak, re-weaver of the world, big-life lover. Re-label yourself and incinerate the old labels."

SARAH

When I first was diagnosed with ADHD, I grieved. A lot of the books I read made it sound so terrible. Those with ADHD were labeled diseased, considered a financial and behavioral burden to their families and the community. Then Alice began to show me how my so-called too-muchness, my Sarah-ness, was also a gift. My impulsiveness makes me creative. My action-oriented nature helps me inspire groups that feel stuck back into inspired action. My sensitivity helps me notice things others don't.

Have you ever been shushed or told you're too quiet (or too loud, impulsive, slow, etc.)? How do you want to re-name your unique qualities and claim them?

Dear God, take away the heaviness of past labels and set me free to be as me as I can be.

SEPTEMBER 23

ELEVATE YOUR PERSPECTIVE

ALICE THE ELEPHANT

"It's important to gain perspective. Climb to a higher elevation, drive to a scenic look-out, take the elevator to the top floor. Spend time in that rarefied air, far above the yes and no, the grind of daily activities, and relentless thinking. You will understand that all is very well. Bring that peaceful, non-binary perspective back down to earth."

SARAH

Some people have a natural ability to see the big picture and not get overwhelmed with all the tiny details. My friend Suzi, an interior designer whose specialty is "healing design," is such a person. She has Eagle as a spirit animal who guides her. She is always undaunted by huge projects with dozens of competing elements: budget, design constraints, regulations, personalities, and staffing needs. Like Eagle, she can tap into a mile-high perspective and translate it for contractors, hospital staff, and others on a team.

How could you use an Eagle-like perspective to find peace?

Dear God, help me see like Eagle so I may bring a higher perspective to everything I do.

BE OUT-THERE

ALICE THE ELEPHANT

"Party harder. By that I mean make dates to get with your people who like the same things you do. Decoupage together, go on sunrise hikes, watch art-house movies. Do things spontaneously but plan things too. Connecting with like-minded humans does you good. Very good."

SARAH

It's not unusual for Alice to repeat the instructions above for connection, and I guess it's no wonder. Our society seems to be going through a period of epidemic loneliness. It takes courage to bid for another person's attention and company. What if they're "just not that into me." Or what if they ask and I'm not that into them? I think the idea that introverts like to be alone all the time needs to be banished. We all do need alone time, but without others in my life I tend toward anxiety, distorted thinking, and dark moods. Something about coming together brings out the best in each of us.

Who would you love to make plans with? What sounds fun to do? Contact them now.

Dear God, help me build a strong posse of peeps I can rely on for connection.

SEPTEMBER 25

VOW NOW

ALICE THE ELEPHANT

"Goad yourself into taking action on the projects, creations, and adventures that matter most to you. Do it! Commit while you're feeling on fire. Book the tickets. That blazing feeling will pass, but by then you will have already begun."

SARAH

YEARS AGO, I NOTICED SOMETHING strange about myself. I would sit around and wonder what I should be working on, until somebody would say, "Hey, why don't you write a piece about that?" or "Why don't you teach a class on that?" and suddenly I'd fly into action. I'd write that piece or launch that class. Being encouraged by somebody to do something gave me motivation and clarity. That led to some great projects. But, more and more, I've begun to figure out what I want to create. I've also learned that I need to goad myself, rather than waiting for somebody else to do it. Committing publicly or buying a (non-refundable) ticket sometimes provides the no way out feeling I need in order to finish the job.

Who goads you to do great things? How good are you at goading yourself to do the things that delight you and matter most to you?

Dear God, help me commit wholeheartedly to the projects and things that matter most.

SEPTEMBER 26

TAKE IT ALL IN

ALICE THE ELEPHANT

"Revel in the delicious delights you stumble onto daily—an incredible person, a kick-ass song, a riveting book, a sublime performance of birdsong, a beautiful vista, a charming dog. Your ability to connect with the ineffable is ridiculous. Lots of people are just having an ordinary day. Dig on what is extraordinary."

SARAH

YOU ARE A SPECIAL PERSON with unique capabilities. Not everyone sees the world as magically as you do. You heart can feel things no other heart can. I'm not sure if you're aware of this, but I hope you're listening. Your skill at sensing what's invisible is powerful. Enjoy it. Share what you see, hear, sense, and notice. Share what you know. This is all a gift for you to deeply enjoy, and it's meant to be shared with others.

How do you catalog the moments of sacredness you witness in your day-to-day life? How could you share what you notice with others?

Dear God, thank you for my gifts, sensitivities, and artistic proclivities. I am grateful and long to use them in your service.

SEPTEMBER 27

GET IT OUT

ALICE THE ELEPHANT

"Use tools you like in order to offload your brain's ideas—voice recorders, apps, lists, color-coded file folders on your desktop, sticky notes. Oof. I know it sounds boring to do this. Surfing is more fun, but this offloading practice will reduce future mental malfunctions."

SARAH

MY BRAIN IS ALMOST ALWAYS thrumming with ideas. Some are sexy and grandiose, and some are more humble. Organize the basement, create a trip to South Africa to connect with animals, create a new offering on my website involving divination and hand-decoupaged chips and call it Shamanic Casino. When this all stays in my head, it can be very distracting. The Notes app in my iPhone is my go-to dumping ground. I try to make a semi-coherent note about the idea, because when the note is less than coherent, I may not remember later what I was so excited about (for example, this recent mysterious note: "Identity shift—ukulele and food"). Sometimes, a short, coherent note can become an incredible three-day retreat.

What feels like a good way to try doing a brain dump today?

Dear God, help me organize all the amazing ideas you send me.

ZIP IT

ALICE THE ELEPHANT

"Shut the front door! Try not to speak, take big action, or make big decisions when you're feeling low. This will prevent many problems. Instead, go to ground and recharge in the base station."

SARAH

ALICE HAS EMPHASIZED THE ADVICE above over the years, whenever I've gone to her in a bit of a panic. "What should I do about... [whatever crisis has arisen]?" Alice always reminds me there's no rush to do anything. Especially if I'm feeling down. It's my job to find my feelgood again before I take action. I wish I could say I have always followed her advice on this. "Going to ground" is Alice's shorthand way of saying, "Get humble, spend time with a tree, scrub the floors, Marie-Kondo the kitchen drawers—but do something to bring yourself back down to earth. From there you'll have better luck."

Have you ever taken big action while in a foul mood? What happened?

Dear God, give me the strength to get quiet and make no moves until I'm in a peaceful place.

SEPTEMBER 29

BE GRACEFUL

ALICE THE ELEPHANT

"If you will dance with life it can be great. Try not to step on toes. When you're the designated leader, lead. If you're not, be leadable."

SARAH

MY PARENTS BEGAN DOING BALLROOM dancing together in their seventies. It's pretty awesome to watch them swirl around the dance floor agreeably. I am awed. Whenever Mark and I try to dance formally, it ends in a hilarious debacle. Both being oldest children, we tend to have bossy tendencies, which is to say, I don't want to surrender to his leadership! They say the way you do one thing is the way you do everything. I have to be careful about trying to lead when I'm not in charge.

What is your usual M.O. in the dance of life—leading or following? What might help you be an even better dance partner?

Dear God, teach me to dance with you.

TRUST YOU

ALICE THE ELEPHANT

"The wild beasties are such good role models for you. They're always listening and paying attention to that beautiful gift: instinct. You have it too! Use it."

SARAH

I'VE BEEN OBSESSED WITH ANIMALS since early childhood. My favorite TV show as a kid was Wild Kingdom, by Mutual of Omaha. I'll always be grateful for the animals who led me back to myself when I had lost sight of my purpose in midlife. The great walrus, beautifully at home in his giant body, surrendered to the sand of the beach, seemed so unworried about absolutely everything. I felt so troubled then and he inspired me. Each beastie seemed absolutely at home in their own skin. I believe that's why they're so irresistible to us. They live innocently and honestly. We can learn to do this too.

Which wild animal fascinates you most? Watch a YouTube video of them today and see what you notice about them. Try to embody that way of being today.

Dear God, help me live innocently and honestly today.

October

OCTOBER 1

LOOK TO WISDOM

ALICE THE ELEPHANT

"There comes a time when a person enters elderhood. The time of running around and making big things happen winds down. If you've done your homework, you will have become a great being. Your only task at this point is to enjoy yourself as much as possible and to spout wisdom. This is the natural order of things."

SARAH

IN OUR YOUTH-OBSESSED CULTURE, A high value is not placed on elders, those who have much more life experience. We humans learned a lot about the wisdom of respecting elderhood during the elephant culls in South Africa (banned in 1995). Elephants were rounded up and the oldest female elephants were killed, because they were no longer fertile. The mistaken logic was that post-menopausal elders were the most expendable. What followed were years of havoc created by violent male adolescent elephants. Those matriarchs who had been killed were the ones who had mentored the young male elephants. In the absence of the matriarch's wisdom, dangerous mayhem ensued.

What would you like to ask your favorite elder? Take them to lunch or pay them a visit (virtual or in person) and learn something!

Dear God, help me learn from my elders.

OCTOBER 2

RELEASE

ALICE THE ELEPHANT

"Let 92 percent of your ideas drift off like dandelion seeds to the wind. Hang onto and nurture the ones that excite you the most. These eight percent may seem ridiculous and illogical, but they always feel like love! They're often so thrilling you can't wait to get started."

SARAH

CERTAIN CREATIVE IDEAS BOOMERANG BACK to me again and again. This happens to all creatives. This idea won't leave me alone! It's good to have a heart for our insistent ideas. Elizabeth Gilbert, author of *Eat Pray Love*, says if you don't use one of these ideas, it may drift to somebody else. Ideas have lives of their own. I know that to take anything worth doing to the finish line, it's going to be a lot of work. So I try to choose wisely.

What idea continues to nudge at you? Who could help you bring it to life?

Dear God, help me sort through the deluge of ideas you gift me with so I may bring the most helpful ones to life.

TRY SUBTRACTION

ALICE THE ELEPHANT

"Sometimes the greatest shift can be realized by removing something rather than adding."

SARAH

One spring, after giving up sugar and flour, I felt a strange emptiness. I had an odd, existential feeling of shrinking that made me feel anxious. The wise person I shared my feelings with asked me, "Sarah, what if it wasn't emptiness? What if it was spaciousness?" My mind was blown. That sounded wonderful! Uncrowded! Unfettered! Possibility! As I allowed the new spaciousness in my body, I began to want to reflect it in our home. I cleared all the furniture out of the front room (sold a few chairs and moved a couch into another room). Then we had a wide open space. Dance studio—yes! Yoga temple—yes! Sometimes I pop up a card table and write in there. In my new emptiness / spaciousness, I found everything.

Where would you like more spaciousness? What needs to be eliminated?

Dear God, help me create room for good stuff in my life by making it clear what needs to be edited out.

OCTOBER 4

SURRENDER IT

ALICE THE ELEPHANT

"Everything, always, is going to be all right."

SARAH

RECENTLY, A DEAR FRIEND'S SON had a troubling symptom. As we waited for lab tests to reveal the cause, I asked Alice to help him (with parental permission, of course). Alice told me all would be well. "But... what do you mean?" I begged her. "Will he be okay? Or do you mean that more existentially?" I was having a hard time letting go. I loved that boy and his parents so much. Then I remembered my God box. It's a papier mâché box with a pair of beautiful yellow birds on it. I wrote the boy's name on a piece of paper, followed it with, "... is completely healed," tucked it in my God box, and went to bed. In the morning, after their doctor visit, the text from his mom came: "He's just fine!"

Designate a God Box for yourself. Put something or someone in there that you're ready to surrender.

Dear God, help me change the things I can and give me the courage to let go of those I cannot.

DETACH

ALICE THE ELEPHANT

"You cannot control the outcome, so just let go. If your creative output somehow pleases you, that is enough."

SARAH

THIS MESSAGE CAME FROM ALICE when I was working on my second book, Born to FREAK. The book is filled with confessional personal stories and salty language. I had a big dream that the book could comfort and inspire others like me, but I felt vulnerable and afraid. What will people think? I worried people wouldn't like it at all or that I would come off as ridiculous. Alice helped me realize I wouldn't be able to finish the book properly until I let go of all those things. I had to be willing to be vulnerable.

Where do you have trouble letting go with your work?

Dear God, I put all the outcomes of my efforts into your capable hands.

OCTOBER 6

CHECK IN

ALICE THE ELEPHANT

"Things do change. It's good to ask yourself every once in a while, Is there anything I'd rather be doing with my life right now? If the answer is yes, you can begin to hatch a fresh plan immediately. The very design of you is expansive."

SARAH

WHEN THINGS ARE GOING PRETTY well in my life, it indicates nothing big needs to change. But small changes often bring delight. Adding a beautiful way to help my clients by using a new spirit song feels wonderful. Scheduling a walk with a new friend brings new connection and joy. Disrupting an old pattern of going to bed too late by creating a new early bedtime routine shifts my energy.

What changes would you like to see in your life at the moment, big or small? How could you take a small step toward this change?

Dear God, thank you for the endless variety of options you offer to shift and expand my experience.

BE YOUR BEST

ALICE THE ELEPHANT

"Confidence settles on you when you realize you're in the process of becoming all that you are. It's never an overpowering feeling. Instead, it's a simple relaxation into this truth: you are doing things you like in the best way you know how."

SARAH

I GOT A CALL FROM A coaching colleague near San Francisco. Would I like to come and give a keynote and run a workshop for her group? Me? I thought. Could I do that well enough that it would be a success? As we spoke about her group, I realized it was a wonderful opportunity. I did have something to offer and I began to be excited about it. The day of the event surprised me. I was a little nervous, but I knew deep down I was doing the best job I knew how. It wasn't perfect, but I experienced the confidence Alice spoke of.

What does confidence feel like to you?
When have you felt the most confidence?

Dear God, help me do my work at the highest level.

OCTOBER 8

BE A GUEST HOUSE

ALICE THE ELEPHANT

"Breathing is one of the most powerful tools you have for feeling your feelings. When anger comes, when joy comes, when grief comes, take deep breaths. Welcome each feeling. Watch them arrive and, eventually, sense them taking their leave."

SARAH

As I lay there, giving birth to our daughter, breathing made the pain manageable. So it is with strong feelings. Rumi's poem "Guest House" has brought me so much comfort, especially during grief. Grief can feel so permanent and awful. Yet, the poem reminds me, each strong feeling is simply a guide sent from beyond to help me. I breathe, as Alice suggests, because it helps me sit with each guest feeling and be in the present moment.

Bring to mind something you've had strong feelings about lately. Add breathing into the feeling. What changes?

Dear God, thank you for my breath and the capacities it allows me.

OCTOBER 9

IT'S YOUR BIRTHRIGHT

ALICE THE ELEPHANT

"That peace that passeth all understanding is not in outer space somewhere. It's not a one-time prize saved for a near-death experience. Nor is it only for a chosen few. It is everywhere and accessible by everyone. Close your eyes and ask for a vision to form inside your heart that will connect you to this peace. Think of this image often."

SARAH

DURING A SHAMANIC HEALING, I once received a gift from the spirits from my friend Kaweah. In the healing, Kaweah told me the spirits had placed a gift of three white roses in my heart. I could feel them immediately. A decade later, just thinking about them brings me peace.

What image comes to you when you close your eyes and ask for a vision to form inside your heart?

Dear God, thank you for the amazing gift of peace I can access anytime I choose.

OCTOBER 10

NO MISTAKES

ALICE THE ELEPHANT

"Remember that you truly cannot make a wrong turn. So keep reaching, dreaming, and acting on those magical impulses."

SARAH

THAT MESSAGE COMES AGAIN AND again from Alice, so I share it here in this book more than once. We are all so beloved. We are not so powerful that we can screw this (or anything) up. All we need to do is get calm and take whatever action feels like the right one to take in the moment. Alice reminds me it is always this simple, despite how much I try to complicate it.

When you get calm, what tiny action is calling to be taken right now?

Dear God, loosen my fears so I may take loving actions toward my dreams.

MAKE SPACE

ALICE THE ELEPHANT

"When a friend or loved one is in pain, breathe for them. Your steady, calm, deep breaths create something akin to an enormous and divine lap for them to rest their weary head on. In your breath, they can find comfort."

SARAH

IT CAN BE SO TEMPTING to offer advice to my children, parents, friends, or my partner Mark when they are struggling. Or to remind them of their strengths. Or to encourage them. But none of those is nearly as effective as my deep belly-breathing. Thank you, Alice.

Who could you breathe for right here, right now?

Dear God, thank you for the sacred power of my breath.

OCTOBER 12

SAME SAME

ALICE THE ELEPHANT

"When you go out into the world each day, remember that, despite how things may seem, every single person you encounter also wrestles with fear, just like you do. Smile, breathe, and do what you can, when you can, to put others at ease."

SARAH

In my mind, there are people who seem so far ahead of me on the path. More together. More centered. More effective. It can be easy for me to forget that everyone (even those who seem exceptionally "successful" or spiritually "accomplished") is just another human being, here traveling on their own journey, working through their own curriculum. When I remember this, I give the same grace to everybody I encounter. Especially the ones who don't appear to need it.

Whom do you admire? Can you perceive how they are human, like you?

Dear God, thank you for giving me all these relatives, brothers, and sisters on this amazing path. Help me be present for each one I encounter.

OCTOBER 13

SLEEP ON IT

ALICE THE ELEPHANT

"You may have a love for the rush. But don't let the chaos-craving part of you (the part that feels most at peace in the eye of the tempest) make a decision that will hurt a relationship, create more difficulty, or destroy a beautiful equilibrium that exists."

SARAH

A PART OF ME IS ALWAYS searching for something new—a new idea, a new place to live, a new transformative adventure. This is a beautiful part of me. I am a visionary. This part of me has helped me find many solutions, learn new things, and explore the world. But I also need to be careful to remember I have a partner and a family. My new idea to make the whole family vegan overnight may not harmonize with their idea of a good time. New ideas are great, but if my roots are too shallow there is a risk of toppling.

Has your love of excitement or novelty ever gotten you into trouble? How so?

Dear God, help me discern which impulses you want me to act on and which ones I should let pass.

OCTOBER 14

EMBRACE THE END

ALICE THE ELEPHANT

"Today is a great day to think about your death. Lie down somewhere cozy. Do a mental run-through, as if it were happening right now. Ideally, who is here with you? As you look back on your life, is anything missing? Don't wait another minute to take action on anything that bubbles up. This is really living."

SARAH

When I think about my death, I mostly think about gratitude and wanting to love people better. You might think about your will, a letter you need to write, a soul dream you haven't acted on yet, caring less about what other people think about you, or giving your Gmail password to your designated power of attorney. All of it is valid. When you're ready to die every day, you're fully primed for life.

If you had died yesterday, what would you wish you had done more of? Less of?

Dear God, help me live fully alive, not half-dead.

SHED YOUR SKIN

ALICE THE ELEPHANT

"When you can't see the forest for the trees, perform a clean sweep of your work space. Dump, delete, and clear the decks, except for current and active ideas and projects."

SARAH

WHEN I'M OVERWHELMED AND HAVE a bit of downtime, clearing the decks is something Alice frequently advises. Snakes do it on the regular, and they don't do it one scale at a time—they lose the whole darn skin in one wriggling shebang. They let go of the unnecessary. It feels so good to make room for clarity.

What workspace (laptop, desktop, dining table, studio, or maybe even your altar) needs a refresh? Commit a block of time to putting it in order.

Dear God, remind me that, in a physical world, I can take physical actions to shift my energy.

OCTOBER 16

PRAYERS UP

ALICE THE ELEPHANT

"Is there something you'd like to change or accomplish that has felt impossible to do on your own? Ask for my help! And pray to the Great Mystery, the Creator, or whomever you pray to that has a power greater than your own. You were never meant to accomplish this (or anything else) alone."

SARAH

When something feels impossible—a project (it's too hard to figure out how to have a card deck printed and sell it myself!), a shift in a relationship (our marriage will never be what I long for it to be!) or a big change you want to make (but I've never been successful in changing my relationship to food, and believe me I've tried!), I first try to admit my helplessness. Next, I ask God to take this thing off my hands and do with it what he can. Last, I like to make a small offering to Mother Earth to thank her for everything and say, "Please help." I offer tobacco or a flower blossom or a bit of food I have cooked. I keep doing this daily until something happens.

Make an offering and pray today. How does it feel? If it feels good, why not keep going with it?

Dear God, thank you for my life. Please help me with everything.

THANK YOU

ALICE THE ELEPHANT

"It's a good idea to build a relationship with the spirits of nature and your home. Call out to the spirit of the land your home sits on. Thank it for the specific support you sense it gives. Then ask it how you can honor it. Tending this relationship enables you to thrive in ways you had not thought possible."

SARAH

THANKS TO ALICE, I'VE MADE many journeys through the years to the spirit of the land our home sits on. One of our past houses said it was happy but it wanted us to do a few things to take care of it—touch up the scuffed paint on the walls and freshen up the plantings out front. Those little actions made our space seem more sacred and the house seemed to sing back its gratitude. Other times, I have learned things like how the stump behind my office is a tree spirit that watches over my work. I make offerings of flowers on the stump regularly to say thanks.

How could you honor the spirit of your home and the land it sits on with a gift?

Dear God, thank you for this sacred land and space you have provided for me to live in.

OCTOBER 18

EXPANSION COMING SOON

ALICE THE ELEPHANT

"Out at the edges of the Universe, neverending active expansion and growth is occurring. It's the same with you! Many of you think you want to be done with your learning and growth, and 'arrive' or be finished. Instead, welcome the change that needs to come next. How do you want to grow right now? What next thing would be amazing?"

SARAH

I USED TO THINK, I CAN'T wait until I... adopt our first child... publish my book... find work I love! Then I'll feel utterly content. But when I arrive "there," I'm already moving on to longing for the next thing. Do you remember when you wanted what you now have? Wanting is what makes life so exciting. If we were complete, we'd have no "work" to do and no exciting adventures to take.

Think of a challenging new growth opportunity ahead of you and be grateful for it.

Dear God, help me be completely willing to do everything asked of me during this season of change in my life.

RECONNECT WITH THE WILD

ALICE THE ELEPHANT

"When you feel lousy, irritable, or otherwise out of sorts, it would be a very good idea to step outside. There in the open air, ask for help. The wind, sun, moon, sky, earth, and water can help you shift and find your feelgood again. If you're stuck in traffic on the New Jersey Turnpike, hang your head out the window (carefully)."

SARAH

WE MAY NOT ALWAYS BE able to step outdoors. Adding a formal forest-bathing session to an already busy schedule is never a useful pressure. But we're never too busy to connect with the earth in some way. Even if you're stuck in a windowless cubicle, you can imagine roots growing out of your tailbone into the cool, rich, dark soil beneath the building. Making this reconnection is often all I need to feel at home again so I can be at ease.

Try growing roots down into the earth right now. How does this make you feel?

Dear God, help me remember that I am part of the family on this amazing planet.

OCTOBER 20

SEE WITH YOUR HEART

ALICE THE ELEPHANT

"Make your decisions from here." (Alice points with her trunk at her heart.) "Not from here." (Alice points with her trunk at her head.)

SARAH

Sometimes, after I've made an inspired decision (I will go do [X]! There! I've put it on my calendar. How perfect!), at a future point, fear comes and I begin to doubt the decision. Confusion arises. I know I always have a choice, but which way should I go? Is that thing I scheduled still a yes or should it be a no? I pray for clarity. What does the Great Mystery want to happen? I also check in with my heart, seeking its guidance. My heart isn't afraid to do hard things. And I trust that whatever choice I make, it's okay.

How do you know whether you're in your head or in your heart?

Dear God, help me find clarity in all my decisions.
Guide me toward what creatively wants to happen.

OCTOBER 21

WOOHOO!

ALICE THE ELEPHANT

"Orgasmic ecstasy is one of the ways the Creator devised to prepare you to open up to divine power. It also prepares you for death, a passageway with the potential for great bliss. Enjoy!"

SARAH

SOME OF US HELPERS, HEALERS, and artists can get so caught up in everything and everyone else that we leave little room for the beautiful and sacred practice of orgasm. I speak from experience. What if what Alice says is true? Best get crackin'!

Is there sufficient space in your life for you to enjoy this sacred gift? What gifts does it deliver?

Dear God, woohoo! And thank you!

HOW GOOD ARE YOU WILLING TO LET IT GET?

OCTOBER 22

LOOK OUT

ALICE THE ELEPHANT

"Your soul is fearless and has an appetite for meaning. Your soul wants to be useful in this world for the highest good. Your ego, however, may have more Kardashian and cashmere-enveloped ambitions."

SARAH

YEARS AGO, AFTER INDULGING MY desire to have an Elle Decor–worthy kitchen, I realized that no environment, no matter how beautiful, could deliver the glory that being useful in the way I longed to be useful could. I could fight it, but the evidence revealed that, for me, the truest riches could only be found in being of service to the divine. This is my truth. I have to stay alert for ambitious thoughts, to be sure they're not taking me on a painful detour away from my truth.

What is true for you about your appetites? Where does your soul find meaning?

Dear God, help me shed my unhelpful ambitions so I may live my truth.

ALWAYS DETACH

ALICE THE ELEPHANT

"Always remember that you are charged with doing the work, but actual results are out of your hands."

SARAH

BEFORE A RETREAT OR AN event, I often fret and worry. What if people come but what I have planned doesn't work, or somebody feels that it made them feel worse, not better? Alice has taught me that the only thing I have control over is my preparation. Have I done everything I need to do to prepare properly? If so, no matter what the outcome, it is okay. I've done my best.

How could you let go of the outcome of an upcoming event or project you may be a bit anxious about? Would you be willing to share with somebody an intention to detach?

Dear God, all my outcomes are yours. Thank you for taking care of them for me.

OCTOBER 24

BE THE CHANGE

ALICE THE ELEPHANT

"Want to change the world right now? Close your eyes. Imagine the most beautiful, lush bouquet you can: peonies, anemones, roses, or stalks of purple lupine. Send this bouquet to someone who needs it. Imagine them receiving it."

SARAH

SOMETIMES EVEN I, SHAMANIC PRACTITIONER and dear friend of Alice the Elephant, can forget that it's just as important to work in the invisible world as it is in the visible. And just as powerful. Try it.

Create your bouquet and send it now.

Dear God, thank you for giving me so many ways to be of service to creation.

RETREAT

ALICE THE ELEPHANT

"Don't forget to steal away from the crowd, and even from your favorite people in the world, for an hour, a day, a week, or a month. Sometimes it's good to choose this aloneness so you can draw closer to me. We can share in the bittersweet ecstasy of silence."

SARAH

I ATTENDED AN ALL-DAY WORKSHOP IN Minneapolis, but halfway through the presentation, I realized that wasn't where I needed to be. I snuck away and went to the local public library. In the library parking lot, I listened to a sweet message from a friend on my phone, answering a burning question I'd had. I went back to my hotel room and meditated and had a sudden breakthrough. Alice and all the other elephants filled my hotel room and comforted me as I sobbed in the ecstatic silence, crying about everything: how hard it is sometimes to be human and how much I love everybody in my life. I was glad for the unhelpful seminar and for the breakthrough I had anyway. It might not have happened at home.

What has been your experience with taking a retreat for yourself?

Dear God, help me give myself permission to do the things I must do to be closer to you.

OCTOBER 26

YOU YOU YOU

ALICE THE ELEPHANT

"You are a supercalifragilistic wonder! There is nobody who can make and do things in the peculiarly fantastic way that you can. Please don't hold back. Your people need you."

SARAH

I REMEMBER ONCE WALKING INTO OUR local bookstore and realizing the shelves were filled with amazing books. Lovely books. Famous books. Brilliant books. Suddenly, I had the overwhelming and very disheartening thought, Why bother to write any more books, Sarah, everybody else is already doing it, and they don't need yours. I went home surrounded by a smog-cloud of self-pity. Later, I asked Alice what my gifts and talents were (with the thought that I certainly didn't need to bother writing any more). She shared the message above. I was encouraged once again and felt safe enough to write some ideas about a new book I want to write someday.

How do you feel when you compare your work to that of others? What changes when you step into the belief that you have a unique perspective and your work is needed?

Dear God, help me live this truth: I have something special to share with the world.

YOU ARE SAFE

ALICE THE ELEPHANT

"Own your point of view. If you're not offending someone, you're probably not being completely authentic. You were born to ruffle feathers. When in doubt, ask if the ruffling is for the greater good. If it's important in the big scheme of your life to express it, then, by all means, express it."

SARAH

AS A LONG-TIME PEOPLE-PLEASER, I'VE freaked when somebody strongly disagrees with something I wrote or said. Deep down, I fear being rejected for my beliefs. Most of the time, I feel like it's best to keep quiet and let God handle things (for example, regarding issues like vaccination versus no vaccination, Republican versus Democrat, Taco Bell versus Taco John's). And, sometimes it's imperative for me to share my point of view, whether people approve or not, like when standing up for justice or for my belief that all humans have a right to practice their spirituality, no matter what.

When have you avoided ruffling feathers and it felt terrible?

Dear God, take my fear of being rejected from me so I may speak my truth.

OCTOBER 28

IT'S NOT A COP-OUT

ALICE THE ELEPHANT

"Don't let anybody tell you that prayer is an excuse for not taking action. Prayer is an action at the level of the spirit—a powerful one. Often, prayer will show you what you need to do (or not do)."

SARAH

When terrible things happen, I often see a call go out on social media to, "Quit saying you're praying and actually do something." It's happened so much recently that I went to Alice to ask her about it. She shared the message above with me. Prayer is real. Prayer is taking action. If you or somebody you care about has ever been prayed for by a friend or your community, you know what I'm talking about. Take action if you feel inspired. If you pray, be confident in prayer's power to accomplish things you could not accomplish alone.

How do you feel when you hear others say that prayer is bogus?

Dear God, thank you for your wisdom and for the way I feel when I spend time with you in prayer.

GET TOGETHER

ALICE THE ELEPHANT

"Spending time with one another is extremely important. There are those of you who will protest, saying, 'I'm not a people person' or 'I'm not like anybody else—I don't fit in with groups.' That attitude will keep you from your purpose. I love you. And that attitude is absolute poppycock."

SARAH

IT WAS MY EGO THAT used to make me want to run away from groups. I'd want people to do things my way, so I'd try to avoid group processes. It's hard sometimes to sit and listen to others. Or I'd think, This isn't what I want to be doing! But a group functions on the idea that the group's overall needs are more important than the individual's need. I lean in now and try to put the group (and all my thinking about it) in God's hands.

What groups have made you uncomfortable in the past? Why?

Dear God, help me find groups I can humbly be a part of so I can learn about relationships.

OCTOBER 30

DON'T WORRY

ALICE THE ELEPHANT

*"When you worry about others, you use your imagination to guess what's going on in their heads and hearts. It's not the worst waste of time, but there are *mucho más mejor* things you could be doing, like tuning in to your own heart. What does your heart need?"*

**much better (Spanish)*

SARAH

THE MINUTE I BEGIN WORRYING, I'm in trouble, because my focus is elsewhere. Instead of being here in my own carcass, living fully, I'm dwelling anxiously on something I have no control over. Day by day, I get better at pointing my attention back to my own beeswax and tending my own destiny. That's the only sphere I can hope to have influence on.

Are you a worrier? What have you worried about this week? Is it something you have any control over, really?

Dear God, please take my worries from me because I cannot manage them.

HONOR THE DEAD

ALICE THE ELEPHANT

"It is so beautiful and important to be remembered after you're gone. Make an artful place in your home for remembering your loved ones and ancestors. Keeping their memories alive on an altar like this helps them in their process and it helps you too. You won't worry so much when it's your time to cross the threshold. The ones you've been remembering will be there to walk you home."

SARAH

I RESISTED THE CONCEPT OF ANCESTORS for a long time. The resistance was my defense of my own sweet family members who were connected not by blood, but by adoption. What if my kids could never know their ancestors? I didn't want to make a big deal out of blood relatives. Alice gently informed me that this was a mistake. My ancestors also include dearly departed friends and chosen family. I try to live my life in a way that honors the lessons they taught me. We are all related. We are all family. Our family altar honors all relatives, blood and otherwise.

How do you honor your dearly departed?

Dear God, help me remember and honor all who prayed me into existence and carried me along.

November

NOVEMBER 1

GRACIAS

ALICE THE ELEPHANT

"Think of money as a big fat thank you. When you receive it, say, 'Thank you.' When you pay it out, say, 'Thank you.' You'll always have what you need."

SARAH

I'VE SPENT A LOT OF time asking Alice about money. She's so wise. She always helps me find a better-feeling place around the money that I earn and spend. When I earn, I say, "Thank you, Creator, for giving me this amazing spirit-work I love to do. My heart is so happy." And when I give money out for spa services, I say, "Thank you for that amazing Turkish bath scrubbing. I feel like a newborn lamb!" When I make a philanthropic donation, I say, "Thank you, Honor the Earth, for dedicating your lives to caring for our sacred waters." When I purchase an album, I say, "Thank you, Amitiel, for spending more than ten thousand hours playing your guitar. Your music bring tears to my eyes!" Being specific in my gratitude helps me tune in to deeper layers of it.

How would you like to give thanks for your money that comes and goes?

Dear God, I'm so grateful to have what I need and to be able to joyfully share it with others.

NOVEMBER 2

REMEMBER

ALICE THE ELEPHANT

"Love where you are. Can't you see that this is everything you have ever prayed for? Why not allow everything, in this moment, to be as it is?"

SARAH

When I visit Alice, sometimes she simply reminds me that the way things are now (and all that I have) is a result of my previous prayers and dreams. I longed for a partner, and I received Mark. I longed for children, and we were gifted with four! I can pray for other things too. If I'm wanting peace and calm, I have the power to relax, to stop striving, to cease arguing with reality and accept what is. When I do that, I remember to breathe. Breathing always brings me swiftly around to gratitude. Sitting here now, breathing is pretty heavenly... even though the dog is starting to hack up a hairball onto the carpet in the other room. The clean-up procedure can wait while I enjoy this moment.

What is present in your life right now, that, at one time, was only a prayer from your heart?

Dear God, thank you for all the answered prayers. I am grateful for every one.

NOVEMBER 3

GRINNING HELPS

ALICE THE ELEPHANT

"If you'd like to make an enormous difference today, smile. Whether anybody witnesses your smile or not is unimportant. It is felt everywhere."

SARAH

SOME DAYS I FEEL OVERWHELMED at the state of the world. I'm desperate to make a difference, but how? It seems nothing short of a grand gesture—a bazillion dollars of relief aid or a million safe-housing units with clean water—is needed. I feel powerless and overwhelmed. Alice always reminds me that whatever I can provide is not inconsequential. A smile. A hug. Kind words. Serving on a community board. Doing my professional work with great attention and care. It all matters.

What would it look like today for you to tend the part of the world within your reach with your own two hands and your heart?

Dear God, show me how to make a difference today.

NOVEMBER 4

HOLD THE VISION

ALICE THE ELEPHANT

"After making a big commitment, doubt and even fear can sometimes arrive. Trust that original moment and try to recall what exactly it was you dreamed of creating or experiencing. Double down in your intention to accomplish that."

SARAH

WE FOUND A PROPERTY FOR a healing studio that felt close to perfect and made an offer. It was accepted. The entire process had felt spiritually guided and amazing. A few days after signing, we discovered that our next-door neighbor-to-be had allegedly committed a violent crime against another neighbor. I panicked. Had we made the wrong decision? I went to Alice. "What the heck? Tell me about this?" She told me not to worry. We decided to stay the course. A week later, the accused neighbor was sentenced to prison and evicted. Our new neighbors turned out to be wonderful. Hold the vision. Trust the process.

When have you had post-purchase or post-commitment dissonance? What were you afraid of? Did you find a way to move onward with your vision?

Dear God, help me hold a vision and trust the process that follows, even if it's challenging. Guide me every step of the way.

FAITH GROWS

ALICE THE ELEPHANT

"When you trust more in the invisible than the visible, you have made progress. The way to get there is by taking notes. When you followed the guidance I gave you, was it helpful? Track your outcomes. If my track record is good, you will have proved to yourself that you can lean on me more."

SARAH

When I first began keeping a diary of my journeys with Mother Bear and Alice, I was very skeptical, but went ahead and recorded follow-up notes. For example, if they gave me advice on my marriage, growing my creative work, or raising our kids, I followed their advice and tracked the results to see if their advice helped. Over time, I learned that assistance from those helping spirits provided better outcomes more than 95 percent of the time! Some of the outcomes were so mysteriously miraculous I could hardly believe it. That was how I grew my faith in my loving and compassionate spirit helpers.

How is your faith in the invisible / divine these days? Would you be willing to track the results of the guidance you receive?

Dear God, help me develop my faith in a way that's powerful for me so I reach a state of trust and relaxation more often.

NOVEMBER 6

BE HERE

ALICE THE ELEPHANT

"Being a reliable friend is one of the greatest gifts you can offer. All you have to do is show up again and again."

SARAH

One time, when I was scared, I asked two friends if they would accompany me on a difficult and possibly very unpleasant mission. To my surprise, they both said yes. They sat on either side of me during the challenging occasion. I remember being astonished at how loved and strong I felt. They showed up for me in a powerful way. Another friend told me the story of a time when she was scared and her friend took her to a church and offered to pray with her. They got down on their knees. Her friend made a plea to God to guide and protect her. Nobody had ever showed up like that for her. It brought her so much peace. She felt so loved.

When has somebody showed up for you in a powerful way?

Dear God, teach me how to tend my friendships. Thank you for the presence of these incredible beings in my life.

LOVE YOURSELF

ALICE THE ELEPHANT

"Every time you encounter a mirror, take a moment to greet yourself by looking yourself in the eye and saying, 'I accept and celebrate you 100 percent.' You might not mean it at first, but with time you'll begin to believe it. Things will get really sweet when that happens."

SARAH

IF EYES ARE THE WINDOWS of the soul, this exercise of Alice's is a sort of shortcut to gazing at our own souls. What I notice when I do this exercise is that I get a funny knowing or a glimpse of a being behind those eyes that I feel like I've known for a very long time. It feels good to befriend myself because, for years (and sometimes it still happens), I was pretty hard on myself.

What do you sense or know when you stare into your own eyes in a mirror? Would you be willing to follow Alice's suggestion above for 30 days?

Dear God, teach me to love myself.

NOVEMBER 8

BE WILLING TO SEE

ALICE THE ELEPHANT

"When you notice someone is sad or upset, it can be tempting to quickly pass on by. It is entirely natural to want to avoid suffering. Whenever you can, turn softly toward such a person. You'll gain their trust, and you'll begin to trust yourself more too."

SARAH

LAST NIGHT, MARK AND I were walking down the street and a disheveled woman, who seemed distressed, began to approach me with one of her hands out. "Do you have any extra change?" she asked. The usual script ran in my head: Should I give somebody money on the street? What if they use it to buy drugs? Normally, I don't have much change. I dug into my pockets and found three quarters. "I just need bus fare," she continued. As I handed the coins to her, she quickly handed me back one quarter. "I'm good. Thanks, sweetie!" (Caveat: when you're utterly depleted and experiencing "compassion fatigue," be sure you restore yourself before attempting to reach out and help others. You are not God.)

Have you ever turned away from somebody who was suffering? How did that feel?

Dear God, help me see suffering through your eyes. Show me the highest actions to take.

DO AFFECTION

ALICE THE ELEPHANT

"Snuggling is a way to pray. When two or more hug or cuddle, it's like drawing closer to the divine. Do it often."

SARAH

OF THE FIVE LOVE LANGUAGES described in Gary Chapman's book The 5 Love Languages, affection is my primary language. I've had to learn to restrain myself with one of our kids, who is not in favor of my somewhat gregarious embraces. When I've gone to Alice to ask her what to do, she said, "Keep trying!" So I continue to offer hugs anyway. A good day for me is when I can get five or more hugs. I'd never thought of hugging as praying until Alice called it that, but it makes perfect sense. In the moment of a hug, hearts and bellies connect. Of course we feel closer to God.

Do you get enough hugs? I challenge you to get / give five by sundown today!

Dear God, help me find as many people and beasties to hug as I can today!

NOVEMBER 10

SHIFT YOUR PERCEPTION

ALICE THE ELEPHANT

"When you breathe, consciously breathe love in. You are immersed in love, but you need to actively perceive this to really know it. Feel this adoration enter your body. Feel it enter every nook and cranny of your carcass and infuse every last cell. This is grace on tap."

SARAH

When I find myself hurtling down the freeway in a big city at rush hour, I'm usually in a sheer panic. Especially if it's road-construction season or a semi-trailer truck is behind or beside me. Gaaaaa! One of my saving-grace maneuvers when panic rises is to breathe in love. I remind myself to let God metaphorically take the wheel (while I try to loosen my death grip on the actual wheel) and I do my love breathing. It always helps.

Breathe love in now. How does that feel? Repeat two more times.

Dear God, make me aware of your presence in every breath I take.

STRONG IN WEAKNESS

ALICE THE ELEPHANT

"No human being is completely free from fear. Even people you hold in high regard experience fear from time to time. The difference is that some people handle fear admirably, which is to say they don't 'handle' fear at all—they surrender it to a power more capable than them."

SARAH

I REMEMBER WHEN I LEARNED THAT somebody who I admired very much was scared to fly on airplanes. I could hardly imagine that person, someone so aligned with spirit and so faithful, ever experienced fear. But she does. She uses essential oils and meditation to get through a flight. Her fear doesn't keep her from making multiple long-haul flights a year. I've learned that the fastest way for me to get out of fear is to say, "Thy will be done." Those three words remind me that I'm not in charge and all will be well, no matter what.

When fear arises, how do you manage it? Would you be willing to ask somebody you admire how they manage fear?

Dear God, I surrender myself and my day into your hands. Do with me what you will.

NOVEMBER 12

YOU'VE GOT THIS

ALICE THE ELEPHANT

"When you say yes to the yodel of your soul, there's no telling what's going to happen next, but you can be sure you are going to have all the help you need."

SARAH

YEARS AGO, MY DEAR FRIEND Suzi and I said to each other, "It would be really cool to go to Africa someday." We weren't sure how. That spring, we threw a South Africa–themed fundraiser for our local Mental Health Center for Youth. It was so fun to decorate and to choose the recipes we wanted to make. A pair of beautiful zebras graced our invitation that I designed. A few months post-party, Suzi's cousin called. Could she come to South Africa to serve on a bride price negotiation team (for a lobola ceremony) for him in six weeks? Of course she said yes and (of course) I went along! We were flabbergasted by how it came together.

Recall a time in your past when you said yes to your soul's yodel. Did you get the help you needed to pursue it? What is your soul calling you to do now?

Dear God, help me trust that whatever calls to me comes with support.

THEY ARE MIRRORS

ALICE THE ELEPHANT

"Every single person you meet is your teacher. So pay attention! If you're pressed for time, simply focus on the people who irritate you most."

SARAH

My mom and I were each filling out our own worksheets from the book Making Friends with Death, by Laura Pritchett. The worksheet asked, "Who are your enemies?" After taking a few minutes to scan back through my life, I said to Mom, "I have no enemies." My mom half-laughed at me with a wry smile. "Oh, yes you do." And I knew immediately who she meant. I was still so mad at that person. They had hurt somebody I knew—in fact, several people I loved and cared about, including me. How easily I'd hidden that fact from myself. There was my work. I had to begin the work of forgiveness, not only for them, but for me too.

Who are your enemies? If you don't think you have any, ask a trusted confidant for their input.

Dear God, help me see where I need to begin to find forgiveness in my heart.

NOVEMBER 14

RETURN TO OWNER

ALICE THE ELEPHANT

"When you're desperate to heal an estranged or strained relationship, begin by letting it go. Let it all be. This condition can restore peace."

SARAH

SOME SHAMANIC SOCIETIES HAVE A concept of soul-stealing. Soul-stealing may sound harsh, but I've learned it's a powerful concept to be aware of. It happens commonly when parents are unable to let their adult-aged kids grow up and move on when they leave home. My shamanic teacher once asked us to drum for a while and ask ourselves if we were holding onto the soul parts of anybody. I was rather surprised to realize I was holding onto the souls of not one, but three people (an old boyfriend and two others). Gads! To release them, I intentionally blew the soul parts I was holding into a stick and buried it in the ground, asking that when the timing was right, they be returned to their rightful owners by the divine. Three days later, one of those three people called me and we had the best conversation we'd had in years.

Put on a recording of some shamanic drumming or rattling and try the exercise above.

Dear God, help me let go of anybody's soul parts I'm hanging onto, so we can both be free.

MAKE THINGS

ALICE THE ELEPHANT

"Stop vacuuming, Windexing, and worrying about the dog hair silently amassing in the corners of the room. Otherwise, what will you have to show for your most precious work—your art?"

SARAH

POET MARY OLIVER SAID (AND I paraphrase here), Hey, I'm a poet and I'm here getting in touch with the divine, so don't be surprised if I'm late, my house is a mess, or we're out of mustard. All of that will wait. Holy communion must take precedence. When the house gets progressively messier and dirtier while I'm busy with my creative work or traveling, I remind myself that when I'm dead, nobody will remember or care that I allowed the cardboard toilet roll tubes to stack up in the bathroom or that I didn't change the sheets weekly. Maybe it's appalling, but I'm letting chaos reign for a few more days. I hope people will remember how my attention to them (and to my writing) made them feel.

What might you accomplish if your creative (or healing or helping) work became your number one priority?

Dear God, help me find a healthy balance with all of my tasks, creative and otherwise.

NOVEMBER 16

CLOSE THE DISTANCE

ALICE THE ELEPHANT

"Why not abandon any activity that creates distance between you and your Creator? Do an internal check during your boozy book club (I'm a recovering alcoholic and this is torture!). Or while binge watching Apocalypse Now (I can't sleep after watching!). Or obsessively following your nemesis' every move on Instagram (Gaaa!). Does your current activity bring you divine connection, and a feeling of belonging and purpose, or does it separate you?"

SARAH

YEARS AGO, I SERVED ON a marvelous community board. I loved it until, suddenly, one spring, I didn't. I found myself at a turning point in my life and desperately needed quiet time to figure out what was happening. I worried people would be disappointed in me if I left the board. A few were, but resigning helped me to begin to open up to a deeper relationship with the Universe and that changed everything. I'm back serving on a different board now and it feels good again.

Is there a commitment that you need to let go of? How could you take a step today toward freeing yourself?

Dear God, help me weed my garden of activities so I may bloom enthusiastically.

INTERVIEW

ALICE THE ELEPHANT

"When you meet somebody you admire, dig a little deeper. Ask them questions about why they believe what they believe. Ask them what advice they would give to you."

SARAH

WHEN I THINK OF POWERFUL matriarchs, a small handful of women come to mind. Some are local. Some are famous. Some are dead. Each has (or had) qualities I admire: a peaceful sensibility, kindness, a confident and heart-full approach. And, of course, there is my own mother, who is masterful at life, appreciating it like crazy. I was lunching with one of my favorite matriarchs when she told me about a time when she was struggling in her early forties. She ran away from home for the weekend, leaving her bewildered husband to fend for himself with their six young children. The weekend was extremely empowering. She reconnected with nature, spirit, and with her own value. After she returned home, she gave their babysitter a substantial raise, against her husband's wishes. It was a turning point for her, and their marriage began to be more of a partnership.

Whom do you admire and what would you like to ask them? Can you make a date?

Dear God, thank you for giving me wise elders and teachers I can learn from.

NOVEMBER 18

LEAN ON ME

ALICE THE ELEPHANT

"Just for the moment, could you try trusting me? Trust that what you perceive in your heart, right now, is spot on? This will make everything infinitely easier."

SARAH

IN THE VERY BEGINNING OF working with my helping spirits (and occasionally now, if I feel extra attached to an outcome), I sometimes balked at what they told me to share with my clients. I'd worry it would sound crazy or wouldn't make sense. But after all these years and all the good that has transpired when I've listened to my helping spirits' advice, I still can get attached to outcomes. Sometimes I feel embarrassed that I'm not more trusting. I try to remember that I'm a human being—and that's not always easy.

Try trusting a small nudge from spirit that you receive today and see where it takes you.

Dear God, teach me how to fully trust in you.

JUST DO IT

ALICE THE ELEPHANT

"Screw mastery. Get out there and give something a go. It's how you learn. Leave other poor sods in the dust who are waiting to do it perfectly. You just did it. Elephants and born to FREAK humans are like that."

SARAH

BEING IMPULSIVE CAN GET YOU a bad rap. In my book, Born to FREAK: A Salty Primer for Irrepressible Humans, I shared the idea that healers, artists, and helpers are often risk-takers, and that's a good thing. The desire to be quickly masterful at something new stops so many people from trying. That won't be you! You're going to be willing to look like a fool (at first), if you want to do something that interests you.

Is there something new you'd like to try (BMX biking, ukulele, Vedic astrology reading or cheese-making)? When are you going to give it a go?

Dear God, give me the courage and humility to try new things so I can grow.

NOVEMBER 20

TRUE LUXURY

ALICE THE ELEPHANT

"There's no shame in loving beautiful and extravagant things or experiences, but don't let pursuing them distract from your purpose, which is to figure out how to both give and receive as much love as possible."

SARAH

I LOVE BEAUTY. AND I'LL ADMIT that a shopping accident I had once on Tracy Porter's website saved my soul. But if I linger too long studying Shetland sweaters in Robert Redford's Sundance catalog—sweaters I do not need at the moment (even if all proceeds go to charity), I will have wasted precious time. Time I could have spent communing with a tree, doing yoga nidra, or painting watercolor circles on paper (which I later add great Hafiz quotes to and hand out to whoever will accept one). Every year, I take myself off all catalog mailing lists, which helps keep me on task.

Were there times when the pursuit of things and money kept you from your purpose? Are there catalogs that need to be canceled now?

Dear God, make me an instrument of your peace.

EMBRACE THE ENTROPY

ALICE THE ELEPHANT

"When the system you so lovingly set up to support yourself begins to feel confining— which, in time, it will—be willing to topple it. By stripping everything carefully back to the bare bones (and maybe even tossing out a femur), you'll discover a new, higher frequency where you can begin again with a new closeness with Source."

SARAH

When my discomfort grows with the way I'm working or how I'm living my life, I try to take a break: a few hours at a coffee shop away from home, a weekend alone. Do I need more space to write on Wednesdays? Would I rather do my coaching on Mondays? Could I try a new offering for my clients? Like emptying a room of furniture, I mentally clear the slate and try to figure out which things to bring back into the room and which ones need to go on Craigslist. I try very hard not to throw out any babies with the bathwater.

How comfortable are you with change? What system, if any, might need to be toppled in your life?

Dear God, help me embrace destruction, the other side of the coin of creation.

NOVEMBER 22

GET AWAY

ALICE THE ELEPHANT

"It's so important to go off and be with yourself, to hear what your soul has to say about everything. Get ye to a Super 8 for a weekend, a parked Airstream at your aunt's house, or sleep in your minivan at the state park. Without this precious time, you can get lost in everybody else's stories about you."

SARAH

SOMETIMES I RESIST LEAVING HOME. I don't particularly want to be in a dingy hotel room on the freeway so I can attend a shamanic conference, or sit in an extremely challenging Vipassana meditation retreat, or even go on a solo writing retreat. But every time I'm willing to sit alone with myself, I gain fresh clarity about where I am and what needs to happen next. At least three times a year is about right for me.

How long has it been since you sat alone with yourself for an extended time? Could you put such a getaway on the calendar today?

Dear God, give me the courage to remove myself from my busy life from time to time so I may reconnect with myself.

LISTEN UP

ALICE THE ELEPHANT

"Steep yourself in media that lights you up. None of it can give you all the answers, and it's your job to discern what's right and wrong for you, but each thing you're drawn to is a messenger that's been sent from Beyond. Listen."

SARAH

When I'm off on a soul vacation, I'll listen to Oprah's SuperSoul Conversations podcast or a great audio book by Dr. Clarissa Pinkola Estés and steep in the thoughts of somebody I admire. Masterclass website offers a fiction-writing course with Judy Blume (the author of my all-time favorite book from third grade: Are You There, God? It's Me, Margaret). It was such a delight to take that class and learn how she writes. It got me thinking of new ideas. I won't have success doing it exactly how she does it, but I take the parts that inspire me and apply them to my own work.

What is your media diet like? How might you like it to change it?

Dear God, direct me to the best media resources to nourish my soul.

NOVEMBER 24

TEND THE UNSEEN

ALICE THE ELEPHANT

"It's good to do work each day in both worlds: the invisible and the visible."

SARAH

THE LAWN NEEDS TO BE mowed! Can't forget to text my kids in college to remind them I love them! Better throw some black-eyed peas in the rice cooker so we have dinner! I've got to sneak in a walk before it gets dark! It can be easy for me to get caught up in the material world. But when I neglect my work in the spirit realm (prayers, meditation, shamanic journeys and offerings), my material world experience gets wonky. And vice versa. There needs to be a balance because both are important.

How well would you say you're currently tending both worlds?

Dear God, I put you first so I may bring your peace into this world.

NOVEMBER 25

IT'S THE CLIMB

ALICE THE ELEPHANT

"A mountain can be a profound teacher for you. Each holds so much potential and such masterful stillness. You don't even need to visit one in person. Simply find one you'd like to study and bring it into your meditation practice."

SARAH

THICH NHAT HANH SHARES A practice where you focus by saying, "Mountain solid...," in order to develop your mind into becoming more still and unmoving like a mountain. I've found it to be powerful. I got to spend a few weeks near the mountain Apu Pachatusan, located in the Sacred Valley in Peru. As light and shadows played across its face all day and vapor manifested and dissipated several times each morning, I began to understand so many things. I saw faces, warriors, mothers, jaguars on its face. It was as if the mountain was capable of becoming anything it wanted to. I call upon this Apu whenever I do spirit work. It has become an ally.

Of all of the mountains in the world, is there one that speaks to you? Bring a photo of it into your sacred space. Introduce yourself.

Dear God, thank you for the majesty of mountains that help us take our consciousness to greater heights.

NOVEMBER 26

TAP IN

ALICE THE ELEPHANT

"The divine and ethereal music of the higher realms is always reverberating around you. All you need to do is stop moving, breathe, and listen."

SARAH

WHY WOULD I AVOID AN activity that, one hundred percent of the time, leaves me feeling more peaceful, clear-headed, and okay about where I am? This is the great mystery of my (occasional) meditation procrastination. I am human.

In what ways do you avoid mediation, prayer, or making time for God in your life?

Dear God, please help me put peace first in my life.

REMEMBER

ALICE THE ELEPHANT

"Your heart is a hummingbird that has memorized the sweetest flowers, and it knows the way home. If I could impress one thing upon you, it would be this: don't be afraid to do the things your heart yearns to do."

SARAH

RECORDING ARTIST INDIA ARIE HAD a breakdown and a breakthrough. She realized that she had been striving to please others for a long time. What she was doing was no longer in alignment with who she was and she was exhausted. She took a year and retreated to the woods to heal. While being away, she got clear on what she wanted to do and how she wanted to do it. Her story really resonates with me. I don't feel exhausted at the moment, but some part of me wants to stop being so busy for a season and commune with nature. Now that I'm aware of that dream, it feels like my responsibility to do something to make it come true.

What is one of your inner dreams? How might you take responsibility for it?

Dear God, help me make my heart's desires a priority.

NOVEMBER 28

GIVE ATTENTION

ALICE THE ELEPHANT

"If you want to make a substantial impact—whether you're making a pot of kitchari for a group cleanse, creating a Moroccan-themed pool party, or conceiving the design for a national monument to Maya Angelou—do it with loving attentiveness and the results will be greater than you could have imagined."

SARAH

SOMETIMES I GET INTO A dither and visit Alice to ask how I can do whatever it is I'm trying to do successfully. She always calmly and patiently explains (again) that I only need to do whatever it is I'm doing with awareness and heart. Whatever it is will be just dandy. I always complicate things. Spirit reminds me it's always simple.

Would you be willing to stop multitasking and give your whole heart and attention to whatever you're working on? What, if anything, would need to change?

Dear God, help me focus all my attention on one thing at a time.

NOVEMBER 29

GIVE IT UP

ALICE THE ELEPHANT

"You can't afford to hold on to that."

SARAH

When somebody's words hurt me, I go out and find a willing twig in the woods and tell it my story. With my breath and intention, I send all my grief pain into the twig, then poke it into the ground (or place it in water), so the earth can receive it. It may sound silly, but try it and see how you feel afterwards.

What did they say that hurt or made you feel small? Go outside and try the procedure above.

Dear God, thank you for Mother Earth, who always willingly takes my pain and mulches it into something useful again.

HOW GOOD ARE YOU WILLING TO LET IT GET?

NOVEMBER 30

TREASURE HOME

ALICE THE ELEPHANT

"Your living space is your cathedral. Why not make it reflect the beauty of the whole of creation. Cherish and tend each element. Gift away what you're unable to revere on the regular."

SARAH

RECENTLY, I REALIZED OUR FRONT porch was looking sad. My daughter Josephine and I took stock of the situation. She sketched out her ideas. We removed a chair. I vacuumed the ancient indoor-outdoor porch carpet and swept the cobwebs from the windows and siding. Josephine found some lanterns and festooned them with holiday ribbon and greenery. She hung a fresh wreath on the door. Since we completed that loving gesture, returning home feels sweeter. I feel more like I have my act together. We've had fun lighting the lanterns when special people return home or come for a visit. Our house is smiling too.

What part of your home could use some TLC? Could you do that project with a helper to make it even more fun?

Dear God, help me cherish my living space.

December

DECEMBER 1

TRUST FULLY

ALICE THE ELEPHANT

"There will come a time when you have complete faith and you trust fully. When this happens, everything will become even more marvelous."

SARAH

I ONCE SPENT TIME WITH ONE of my teachers' teacher, a shaman, in the jungle in Peru. He was extremely kind and humble and had a wicked sense of humor. He alluded to the fact that he already possessed the type of trust in God that Alice references. It didn't mean that he no longer encountered difficulties, but that he was able to be more untroubled by his circumstances than ever before. He shared a harrowing story about a bandit who held him at gunpoint one night. He was afraid, but God instructed him about what to say. As soon as he spoke the words, the mercenary put the gun down. The shaman was able to pitch the gun deep into the jungle darkness and run to safety.

If you had a fully trusting faith now, what might be different today?

Dear God, I put my life in your hands today.

DECEMBER 2

LIVE FREE

ALICE THE ELEPHANT

"Freedom comes when you live from your heart. That's all you have ever wanted."

SARAH

ONE NIGHT I HAD A dream about a pride of lions. I was about to head off into the savannah with several other of the females. Though I was not a lion in the dream, it felt entirely natural to be going with them. Suddenly, a male lion appeared and registered his disapproval of me joining those lions. When I awoke, I wondered if the dream was about patriarchy, or perhaps about my fear of not being qualified / belonging. I shared it with a teacher of mine who said, "I think it's a dream about freedom." That resonated a lot. Freedom to be myself. Freedom to follow my heart. Freedom from my mind (and all of its unhelpful thinking).

What would it look like if you were truly free? How would it feel? What is the first thing you would do?

Dear God, show me how to live free, guided by my heart.

DECEMBER 3

YOU ARE QUALIFIED

ALICE THE ELEPHANT

"You are the manifestation of God consciousness and, as such, you are eminently qualified to be a conduit of wisdom and healing. The only requirement is to continually seek peace."

SARAH

DURING MY SABBATICAL FROM MEDICINE, I realized I wanted to become a healer. I really had no idea how to become such a person and worried a lot that I was misguided or that it might not be possible. Who was I? During that time, I ran into Marianne Williamson's wonderful words: "Our deepest fear is not that we are inadequate. Our deepest fear is that we are powerful beyond measure. It is our light, not our darkness, that most frightens us. We ask ourselves, 'Who am I to be brilliant, gorgeous, talented, fabulous?' Actually, who are you not to be?" They resonated so much. Slowly, little by little, I became willing to sit with myself and a seed of peace began to grow in me. I keep busy watering it.

How will you water the seed of peace within you on this day?

Dear God, make me a conduit for your love and understanding.

KEEP IT TOGETHER

ALICE THE ELEPHANT

"When somebody is bitter, sarcastic, or otherwise miserable, rather than react to them, respond with deep, cleansing breaths. Hold your own sacred ground. Someday, somebody may do the same for you."

SARAH

I WAS AT AN EVENT AND the organizers were hell-bent on getting a photograph of our huge group. It was taking a lot of time. Next to me, a woman complaining bitterly about the process. She was irritated it was taking time away from the gathering's purpose. I had similar thoughts, but, thankfully, my inner voice said, Calm down, Sarah. You have all day for this is. This photo session is sacred too. I have been that bitter lady. I no longer want to be. So instead of adding to her miserable commentary, I breathed deep breaths instead.

When others around you are cranky, breathe for them.

Dear God, give me patience with others.

DECEMBER 5

GOD IS HERE

ALICE THE ELEPHANT

"When I was once a very young elephant on Earth, we were crossing a flooded river in the springtime. I was swept away in the strong current and went under water. While I was submerged, God told me not to worry, and that I would be okay. The next thing I knew, I was far down the river approaching a strange bank. Exhausted, I crawled out and cried for my mother. In time, she came. God was watching over me and he is watching over you too."

SARAH

I REMEMBER FELLOW AUTHOR AND COACH Susan Hyatt telling a group about the time she was sexually assaulted at knifepoint in broad daylight in her neighborhood. God spoke to her during the assault and told her, "This will not define you." Despite that atrocity, she became a huge force for good and has empowered thousands of women. After a debilitating head injury, my Cardiologist friend Kathleen was so angry, wondering why she had survived the accident. God sat at the foot of her bed and lovingly explained to her that she had work to do still on Earth. What Alice is sharing and what so many others have shared with me is that God is always with us.

Do you believe God is watching over you? Or would you be willing to "act as if" that's true?

Dear God, remind me that I'm never alone and that you can speak to me directly or through any method you chose.

DECEMBER 6

BE AWARE

ALICE THE ELEPHANT

"Be still just for a few moments. See if you can perceive all the beauty, absolute potential, rejoicing, cellos warbling, and flowers blooming in the sacred silence. This non-ordinary aspect of consciousness is always here, awaiting your awareness."

SARAH

LIFE IS SO COMPLICATED, AND yet the remedies Alice suggests are always profoundly simple. When I still myself, I can hear Oliver the pug's exquisite snore, the cars softly rumbling by outside, the warm and subtle throbbing of blood moving through my fingertips. There is nothing the matter and everything is beautiful just as it is.

What do you notice when you drop into silence right here, right now?

Dear God, remind me to become still today so that I may find peace.

DECEMBER 7

BE WILLING

ALICE THE ELEPHANT

"If you have said yes to your hero's journey, you can expect your path to be paved with great growth opportunities. Many of them will feel scary and probably be unpleasant. But remember what you've been praying for and be willing to face whatever lies between you and your wish."

SARAH

IT WAS ELEVEN AT NIGHT and we were sitting in candlelight in a screened-in bungalow in the Amazon. The shaman got out his bottle of sacred plant medicine and said to us, "You didn't come all this way not to do some big healing work." I knew he was prepping us for a powerful and, I worried, possibly overwhelming night. I gulped and my stomach lurched at the idea. I preferred to be in control. But, like he said, I wasn't there to be a bystander. I wanted to learn as much as I could and he was my teacher. I sat up tall and drank the enormous cup of medicine he offered me.

What challenges are you facing on your hero's journey? How could you lean in rather than resist in fear?

Dear God, remind me that everything is trying to help me grow. Help me become willing.

DECEMBER 8

BE GENTLE WITH YOU

ALICE THE ELEPHANT

"Sometimes the most important apology is the one you make to yourself. You can be awfully hard on yourself. Can you sit with your younger self and share with them how you wish you would have handled things differently? This tender act toward yourself will begin to bring more magic back into your experience."

SARAH

I'VE NOTICED THAT WE ARTISTS, healers, and helpers can have a tendency to be extremely self-critical and demanding of ourselves. I think this is the attempt of our ego to harden us against the challenges of life. But what might be possible if we were generous with ourselves instead? If we granted ourselves full permission to be human? To feel all of our feelings? To make mistakes?

What past transgression do you still berate yourself for? Would you be willing to take the first step toward forgiving yourself right now?

Dear God, show me where I need to offer myself forgiveness.

DECEMBER 9

REJOICE IN ALL OF YOU

ALICE THE ELEPHANT

"When you feel stabby from shame, stubbornly commit to loving yourself anyway. The more you can stop resisting what is, the greater the opportunity for you to develop new behaviors that make you proud."

SARAH

THAT ADVICE FROM ALICE, WHICH I received years ago, led me to a practice of shouting (out loud), "I love that about me!" whenever I noticed something I felt ashamed about. The way my closet predictably became impassible after I had been working on a big creative project. The way I complained about an esteemed colleague to a friend. The way my car would get so filled with detritus that I cringed whenever I had an unexpected passenger. Each time I accepted my behavior, I realized good things too. Creativity (not a tidy closet) is a priority for me. Yay! I still feel hurt by what happened at work (good to know). I am living an extremely fulfilling and busy life and sometimes I don't choose to make time for car-cleaning. That encouraged me.

Where in your life did you most recently feel a pang of shame? Reflect on why you did what you did.

Dear God, help me to accept myself as I am and improve my behavior wherever possible.

LET IT BE EASY

ALICE THE ELEPHANT

"Having a 'take it easy' attitude with everything is paramount. Never shy away from daunting challenges, but take action with an attitude of tranquility."

SARAH

EVERY TIME I READ MARY Oliver's poem "Wild Geese," I think to myself, Mary Oliver must really know me. I sometimes do feel like I've got to crawl on my knees for hundreds of miles, repenting in the desert. There's a part of me that's determined to lunge at life, demanding more of myself out of some sense that I can never do or be enough. But this attitude I tend toward fills me with dread. Instead, whenever I do as Alice suggests, things get better. I still have difficult steps to take, but I don't need to make them more difficult with my attitude. I can progress with gentleness.

Where in your life do you feel like you're crawling on your hands and knees through the desert? What would it be like to take it easy instead?

Dear God, help me cultivate ease in myself.

DECEMBER 11

BRING IT

ALICE THE ELEPHANT

"Your ultimate assignment is to bring heaven down to Earth. You're going to need to develop a sense of supernatural awesomeness through sweetening activities like nuzzling baby animals, floating in a warm bath with rose petals, and lying beneath wise trees on a warm, breezy afternoon. Do you feel me?"

SARAH

We are capable of becoming lovely conduits of heavenly goodness. According to Alice, we are charged with a daunting responsibility: to do some things that feel very, very good so we may broadcast that good feeling.

When was the last time you did something that felt really delicious? Gold stars if it was five minutes ago. If it's been longer than a week, then get cracking!

Dear God, remind me that you designed me to have the experience of feeling good.

HONOR LIFE

ALICE THE ELEPHANT

"Sit straight. Walk tall. This is the polite way to meet God. Be ready at all times."

SARAH

THIS LITTLE INSTRUCTION FROM ALICE is so profound—for living and for dying. Sitting straight and walking tall bring an attitude of confidence in my ability to be of service, with God's help. It's not about me. It's about honoring the greater power.

Do you feel ready to meet God in this moment?

Dear God, help me be resilient and empowered so I can meet you properly.

DECEMBER 13

YOU'RE EVERYTHING

ALICE THE ELEPHANT

"Your fear of being insignificant is so erroneous. If you could feel the great essentialness of your presence, you'd trade your despondency for rapture."

SARAH

When I was in my twenties, I disliked living in a big city because nobody smiled back at me like they did in my home town. I worried that if I died suddenly (piano falling out of a window and crushing me?) in the middle of a city, nobody would care. Alice reminds me that all this worry is a load of bunk and a faction of my ego. I now cheerfully remind myself that even if I get flattened by a cement mixer in Poughkeepsie, I matter.

When have you ever felt insignificant? Where might you be feeling insignificant in your current life? Imagine how a smile might help.

Dear God, thank you for giving me a one-of-a-kind position here on Earth. I will do my best today to carry out your mission.

TAKE GOOD CARE

ALICE THE ELEPHANT

"I see you sweatin' to the oldies, counting steps, eating a rainbow of vegetables, and imbibing restorative elixirs like your life depends on it. Why not tend to your mind with the same feverish enthusiasm? The mind is not visible like the body is, but if left unattended, it too can become a liability. Given just fifteen minutes of golden silence daily, your mind will become more reliable."

SARAH

IT TOOK ME TEN YEARS of saying, "I want to go to a silent meditation retreat," before I actually attended one. Why? I think it was because the idea of silent meditation seemed so utterly unproductive. Wouldn't it be better to go to a workshop and learn something tangible? Attending a silent retreat (Vipassana) turned out to be one of the best things I'd done in years. I learned something: my mind has a habit of taking me on crazy, wild-goose chases. I'm so much more aware of my unconscious patterns now. Silence, it turns out, is golden.

How strong is your commitment to train your mind when compared to tending your physical body?

Dear God, thank you for my mind. I'm willing to do what it takes to cultivate stillness.

DECEMBER 15

SEEK THE UPSIDE

ALICE THE ELEPHANT

"When you're able to celebrate your particular and precious life, in its present condition, everything will automatically begin to get sweeter. Train yourself to search tirelessly for all that is good."

SARAH

HERE'S A PROCESS THAT HELPS when my brain is in a tizzy and craving things (I must have that new, even fancier coffee maker, those sparkly earrings, those more chic snow boots). I might want those things, but I certainly do not need them. Gratitude dissolves cravings. It helps me to remember that there was a time when I wanted everything I currently have. Wow! Thank you for this modest house, which allows us the freedom to travel. Thank you for the beautiful cedar and apple trees that surround us with their beauty. Thank you for this amazing work I'm so fortunate to do and these clients that somehow find me, inspire me, and touch my heart so much.

Is it easy for you to find things to celebrate about your current life conditions? Name three things now.

Dear God, help me see my whole life through your eyes.

GO FOR IT

ALICE THE ELEPHANT

"Think of those school science films with all the spermatozoa racing furiously toward the egg to fertilize it. This is a powerful metaphor of how badly life wants to be lived though you. You can be a conduit for that purposeful forward motion for the benefit of creation, or you can block it. It's a choice."

SARAH

WHEN I'M AT MY VERY best, I feel a bit like one of those strong swimmers Alice refers to—courageous, enthusiastic, and guided toward my destiny. Other days, I feel less vigorous. On those day, I do a self-check: What's going on with me? What do I need? A simple, 20-minute nap or a phone call connection may restore me. Sometimes those days happen because I'm holding back out of fear. For example, the fear that I will not meet somebody's expectations. If I can spot the fear, I reassure the frightened part of me that she's safe and resume swimming strong, bringing the possibility of something great being created.

Are you feeling like a "strong swimmer" these days? What could bring you more courage and enthusiasm?

Dear God, help me find the courage and enthusiasm to fully let you live through me.

DECEMBER 17

GETTING TO KNOW YOU

ALICE THE ELEPHANT

"There are so many ways to explore who you are! Take personality tests, study your birth chart, print out your numerology profile and pin it to refrigerator door. None of them is the absolute truth, but each offers clues to you, along with opportunities and inspiration."

SARAH

WE WERE ALL GATHERED AROUND a dinner table when a friend brought up numerology. I had an app. Suddenly, I was furiously entering people's names and birthdates and texting them their reports. We had so much fun laughing as we read our reports aloud. I don't let numerology rule my world. I take the bits that inspire and work with them. For example, discovering that my destiny number is three—the number of self-expression, creativity, and social contacts—reassured me. Those are all things I'm naturally drawn to!

What have you learned about yourself from doing such evaluations? Is there a type of assessment you'd like to take? If so, how about taking it today?

Dear God, give me the tools I need to know myself deeply so I can make better choices.

GIVE IT TIME

ALICE THE ELEPHANT

"When something terrible happens, it also means that something else in your life is about to be upgraded. It can take time for that upgrade to be revealed."

SARAH

A MAN CRASHED HIS MASERATI, HIS wife served him divorce papers, and he got fired. All in one day! My mentor and spiritual teacher Martha Beck says that when everything seems to be going to hell, it's a sign that God is calling. If you're willing to face whatever is happening, ask for help, and deal with it, whatever is happening will bring profound blessings. This isn't about spiritual bypassing; it's about seeing the wholeness of a situation. It can be powerful to look at one of the best things in your life (a partner or a BFF) and go backward until you discover a difficult challenge related to it. For example, our amazing family was formed by adoption (beyond-words incredible!), which only happened after Mark and I struggled with infertility (devastating, humiliating, and isolating).

Your turn! What horrible things brought the best things into your life? Keep a list of these. It will help you grow your "willingness" muscle.

Dear God, help me trust that all will be well, no matter what.

DECEMBER 19

MIX IT UP

ALICE THE ELEPHANT

"You were not created to do the exact same thing in the same way every day for the rest of your life. That's what robots are for. Innovate. What could make your work even sweeter today? Try a new color, like cobalt blue, a new time of day, like 6:00 p.m., a foreign ingredient, such as Chinese five-spice, or a new method, like writing with your non-dominant hand."

SARAH

SOME OF MY FAVORITE SHAMANIC teachers are the ones who never, ever do the same thing in the exact same way when they work. Sure, there's always a thread in their work that helps you know whose work it is, but they are never stale. They bring a new drum. Try out a new joke. Add a new verse to a song they've written. They change up the elements and always keep me guessing and delighted.

When was the last time you innovated? What's something new you'd like to try today?

Dear God, show me how to bring newness to my daily work and life.

NEVER LESS THAN

ALICE THE ELEPHANT

"Don't confuse love with kowtowing. Love is a mutual appreciation. You ought never be submissive to another human. There is only one true authority."

SARAH

I WENT THROUGH A FUNKY PERIOD when I believed, because of some guilty feelings I had, that I should surrender to and serve Mark, somehow. It sounds kind of crazy / hilarious now that I'm writing it, but I'm just saying, it happened. During that period, I decided I'd try to please him by making special meals for him and, in my own weird way, put his needs above mine. Of course, it backfired. Mark thought my strange new gourmet, happy-homemaker persona was kind of creepy. And I felt resentful that he didn't appreciate my June Cleaver impersonation efforts. We reverted to mutual respect and our relationship instantly improved.

Is there anybody you take a subservient role with? If so, is it working for you?

Dear God, remind me that you're the only one I bow to.

DECEMBER 21

USE IT

ALICE THE ELEPHANT

"Some of you will have to travel far from home to find what you most want to know. Some of you will find it closer to home. But as soon as you find it, stop seeking and put it to work in your life. This is the secret to good living."

SARAH

A FEW YEARS AFTER STUMBLING ONTO the shamanic path, I became curious about the meditative yogic tradition and I travelled to India on a pilgrimage, where I was initiated into a particular tradition and received a mantra for my meditation practice. I was really enjoying that practice while traveling. Then, one night, we entered a temple with the group's guru. I suddenly felt extremely uncomfortable and knew intuitively that I had to leave. My soul wouldn't let me stay. That tradition and its guru were not for me. As I walked back to my tent, I realized I didn't need another tradition. I already had Alice and all my other helping spirits and a way to connect to the divine. Since that day, I've still enjoyed learning, but I've stopped seeking.

Are you still seeking or have you already found what you were looking for?

Dear God, guide me to the best teachers so I may learn the truth I yearn for.

NO FEAR

ALICE THE ELEPHANT

"Never be afraid to approach someone who is dying. If you listen carefully, I will instruct you. You may also learn from the one who's preparing to transcend. As each of you approaches this threshold between worlds, you automatically become powerful teachers for all present."

SARAH

IT WAS SEVEN IN THE morning. I had felt called to visit my friend Karen, who was dying of ALS and had just checked into a hospice house. When I arrived at her bedside, she was in good spirits and seemed to be comforting everybody around her as they wept. When I asked her how she was feeling, she shared this story with me: "When my dad was dying, I was a little scared and asked him if he was afraid to die. He told me, 'Karen, why would I be afraid? There is absolutely nothing to fear.' Since he told me that, I've never been afraid to die." She received a beautiful gift from her father. He was her teacher. And she was mine.

Whom have you lost and what did you learn from them?

Dear God, take away my fear of dying so I may live fully.

DECEMBER 23

HEART GARDEN

ALICE THE ELEPHANT

"Imagine that your heart and lungs are stuffed with old-fashioned cabbage roses in soft shades of pink—a cardiopulmonary altar of fruity, sweet spiciness. Breathing in, you bless yourself with this essence. Breathing out you bless those around you."

SARAH

ALICE ONCE HELPED ME PROVIDE a distance healing for somebody with pneumonia. She shared a similar image to the one above, but with an abundance of different, multicolored flowers. After Alice provided the healing, I found an artist's depiction of that very image (anatomic images of lungs collaged with amazing flowers). I sent it to the person who was ill, hoping it might inspire her respiration. Thanks to the grace of God, she recovered. I like to do Alice's suggested exercise above when I'm waiting for somebody at a restaurant or when I'm in an audience and we're waiting for the curtains to open. It feels so good.

Try the suggestion above from Alice. Sense the softness of the petals and the spicy, sweet scent. How do you feel?

Dear God, remind me I can be a walking, talking altar and share your blessings with others.

TEND LIFE

ALICE THE ELEPHANT

"Can you imagine not being willing to let a laboring mother into your home when she knocked? Instead, you directed her to an unheated, unwelcoming shed behind your house? This is part of the powerful mythology of the Christmas story. You must wake up and tend life, no matter how busy or exhausted you have become. This is how light can enter the world."

SARAH

WHILE GROWING UP, I NEVER understood that the stories in the bible were also symbolic. Decades later, during a powerful shamanic ceremony, in a particularly challenging moment for the group, I suddenly saw a brand new baby appear in my visions. In the ceremonial space, there was crying from the participants and some were simply curled up in misery. In my vision, the new baby sat looking at all of us, expectant. Would we be able to tend to him? Could we set aside our dramas and suffering and welcome him? It was such a poignant vision and I understood, for the very first time, the true meaning of Christ being born. The baby seemed to represent life itself.

How could you set aside your own dramas and suffering to tend life today?

Dear God, help me find the strength to turn toward what needs my attention today.

DECEMBER 25

GET CLOSE

ALICE THE ELEPHANT

"Imagine you're dancing with me cheek to cheek wherever you go. What could be better?"

SARAH

I MUST ADMIT THAT EVERYTHING IS always better when I call upon Alice or decide to consciously connect with my higher power / God / The Great Mystery. Each offers me a different loving and strengthening perspective.

Would you be willing to dance cheek to cheek with the divine (or one of your spirit helpers or animals) for the next five minutes?

Dear God, help me remember that you are always only a thought away.

DECEMBER 26

KEEP IT SIMPLE

ALICE THE ELEPHANT

"You don't need much. A bed to sleep in. A table for writing. And remember all of it will be gone surprisingly fast, along with you. Don't get lost in collecting property and things. Only love is everlasting."

SARAH

I HAD A VISION ONCE, DURING a plant-medicine ceremony, of a bare room with only a woodstove, a table and chair, a bed, and a small kitchen. The message was that anything more was complication. It inspired me to simplify (yet again!) our home and possessions. My dad is already a master of minimalism. One year he called me over to help him organize his new office. He had about eight objects in his office (plus a few papers in files.). We arranged them on his shelves together. They were a few important photos, some art that had meaning for him, and a model of a wooden sailboat. This year he decluttered and I got the sailboat.

If you pared your life down to the essentials, what would need to go? How could you bless it and pass it on to somebody who needs it more?

Dear God, help me focus on the things I can do to contribute to lasting goodness.

V

DECEMBER 27

WISDOM IS EVERYWHERE

ALICE THE ELEPHANT

"Keep your eyes wide open. Notice the wine-colored apples on the bent bough, the still rabbit beneath the hostas, and the flattened grass where the deer slept last night. All offer their advice to you."

SARAH

If there is one Beastie who has taught me the most about attention, it is Jaguar. Jaguar shows me how much I can learn by simply watching and using all my senses—how much I can accomplish by simply being; how much everything is saying to me without uttering a word.

When do you pause to listen for what the things and beings around you are saying to you?

Dear God, wake me up so I can see and hear everything I need to.

STOP ARGUING

ALICE THE ELEPHANT

"You're in the process of learning how to trust. Practice letting me guide you every step of the way. If you're always arguing, it's hard for me to help."

SARAH

WHEN I BEGIN TO WORK with a person who longs to have a trusting relationship with the spirits or the Universe (or God), they are often frustrated. After a few shamanic journeys that leave them feeling more peaceful and calm, they'll say, "But how can I know if this is even real? What if I'm making all of this up?" I tell them, "Test the wisdom the spirits share with you. If they tell you, 'Stop doing so much and get quiet,' then apply their advice to your life immediately. Like a scientist, notice what your results are. If good things unfold, why not keep going? The only proof is in your experience. If the spirits have helped you, then you know."

How is your faith these days? Do you trust the guidance you're given?

Dear God, teach me how to trust.

DECEMBER 29

NAME IT

ALICE THE ELEPHANT

"When you feel scared, acknowledge your fear by stating it out loud. For example, 'I am terrified of three lanes of cars all moving at seventy miles per hour! I'm afraid I'll be obliterated or, at the very least, horribly maimed.' It will make things easier. Try it?"

SARAH

THIS ALICE TIP HAS HELPED me a lot. Sometimes when I state my fear aloud ("I'm scared of my literary agent's power. If she doesn't support a project, I'm sunk."), I suddenly realize after hearing myself say it that it's not really true. The fear balloon suddenly deflates. My fears are frequently quite silly. "I'm feeling scared that a bunch of strangers have the wrong idea about me and my work." Why do I care so much about the opinions of strangers? The world will not end if, in fact, a few strangers are confused about me.

What are you afraid of most right now? State it out loud. Does it seem legit? If so, how could you get support for yourself?

Dear God, help me be aware of my fears and be willing to take inspired action despite them.

BELIEVE TO RECEIVE

ALICE THE ELEPHANT

"Act as if it's going to happen and be willing to entertain fun alternatives."

SARAH

IN COLLEGE, I HAD A dismal score for the physics component of the MCAT (the exam that was used for medical school admission). Because of that, I was told my chances for admission were slim. I decided to apply to my preferred medical schools anyway, hoping I'd get in, but also willing to become an investigative journalist or professional chef if it didn't happen. Not only did I get into medical school, but against all odds, I was accepted by one of the more prestigious medical schools in the Midwest. Self-publishing my first book seemed similarly impossible. I didn't know an ISBN from a pickle fork. Still, I loved books and had a deep yearning to make one. As I put one foot on the gas pedal and slowly began to wobble forward on each of my Hero's Journeys, the helpers appeared, one by one, just like Joseph Campbell promised. They always do.

What's a big thing you want to accomplish? How could you "act as if" it's inevitable?

Dear God, teach me to shoot for the moon and graciously move toward it.

YOU CAN'T MAKE A WRONG TURN

ALICE THE ELEPHANT

"Beneath all the circumstances, thrashing, and endless overthinking, you are peace. To explore this neverending tranquility, put one hand on your heart and the other on your lower tum-tum, just beneath your belly button. Close your eyes and breathe for a while. Once you've tasted a spoonful of this harmony, you'll be in a damn good position to make a decision."

SARAH

I'M OFTEN IN A STATE of non-presence: worried about the future or cringing about the past. It's rather unpleasant. With awareness, however, I can refocus into the present, which is always—despite whatever hell or high water may be on my radar—much nicer. A nifty way to do this is to simply follow Alice's instruction above. Once you have your hands in position, feel the spaces within your heart and pelvis. Really sense that openness, from the inside out. Good! Now, add a few more deep breaths.

What decision do you need to make today? Try making it from your heart and your tum-tum.

Dear God, guide me, moment by moment, where you'd like to me to be.

HELLO DEAR READERS!

I'd be so grateful if you'd be willing to leave a brief review at Amazon, share the book with your beloveds on Goodreads, or gift a copy to somebody who you think would enjoy it.

Thank you so much for your support!
It means the world to me.

With BIG love,

Sarah

P.S. On my website, you can learn about how we can work together one-on-one (I offer shamanic healing and life coaching virtually and in person) and about my trips and events.

FOLLOWYOURFEELGOOD.COM

Thank
You

ABOUT
SARAH BAMFORD SEIDELMANN

I was born of two rather Bohemian individuals and raised in the harsh and tundra-like (warmish for six weeks in the summer) conditions of northern Minnesota with my only sibling, Maria Bamford, a successful stand-up comedienne.

I practiced as a board-certified physician specializing in surgical pathology in a multispecialty group known for excellence in the Midwest. Although I thoroughly enjoyed my wonderful practice and partners, after 20 years in the world of allopathic medicine, I felt a strong pull to do transformative work and to be creative again. By that time, I had four children and my life had become "complicated." I got coached and found it life-changing.

My husband and I decided to right-size our lives by selling off our vacation home and decamping from a 6000-square-foot house into a lovely, more modest one. Then I took a six-month sabbatical from my job as a physician. I found myself wandering deep into the woods. I was re-awakening my own deep connection to nature and to myself. At the end of the sabbatical, I determined that my path was to continue in the field of personal transformation. If you're curious about my vocational transformation from MD to shamanic healer, I wrote *Swimming with Elephants: My Uexpected Pilgrimage from Physician to Healer for you.*

I have a deep appreciation for nature and use many different methods to help others connect to their own brilliance, including animal totems (and other shamanism-based tools, such as journeying and divination), surfing, and forest bathing. I believe that forging a connection to a spirit animal is powerful and wrote *The Book of Beasties: Your A-Z Guide to the Enlightening Wisdom of Spirit Animals.*

Part of being me involves having many, many interests and an extreme curiosity about many things. I was diagnosed as an adult with Attention Deficit Disorder, inattentive type. Getting that diagnosis was a gift, as it helped me fully embrace my irrepressible muchness and my special talent for taking seemingly unrelated ideas and creating something new. I have the ability to hyperfocus and, as a result, enjoy transcendent experiences on a pretty regular basis, which is pretty cool! I also have to be sure to get support and lots of rest so I don't become overwhelmed. I think nature holds the cure to whatever seems to be causing us to struggle, suffer, or feel stuck. I wrote the book *Born to FREAK: A Salty Primer for Irrepressible Humans* to help others diagnosed with ADHD, Asperger's, depression, anxiety, bipolar, and addiction.

First and foremost, I encourage you to re-discover your own FEELGOOD and follow it. It will take you to good places.

DON'T STOP NOW!

PURCHASE THE FEEL GOOD CARD DECK AT FOLLOWYOURFEELGOOD.COM

"How Good Are You Willing to Let It Get? *is guaranteed to lift your mood, put a spring in your step, and pull you out of whatever funk that old logical brain of yours has plunged you into at any given moment. We all need help keeping our vibration high so that life gets better and better. And we all need validation for when things aren't so great. This book and card deck are designed to assist with this level of human homework. Enjoy them.*"

Christiane Northrup, M.D., New York Times best-selling author of ***Goddesses Never Age, The Wisdom of Menopause,*** **and** ***Women's Bodies, Women's Wisdom***

A deck of 60 spirit-infused divination cards created by shamanic healer and author Sarah Bamford Seidelmann MD and her magnificent spirit animal Alice the Elephant. Each elegant card, featuring fantastic images from the public domain and Sarah's personal ephemera collection, is designed to inspire and encourage creatives, healers and helpers of all sorts. Alice offers her sacred wisdom in a lighthearted (and sometimes salty) way and Sarah adds a thoughtful prompt and simple daily prayer to accompany her message. Themes include prayer, meditation, humility, moderation, self-love, family, friendship, creativity, pitfalls & quagmires, addiction recovery, and dealing with fear. **How good are YOU willing to let it get?** We hope that your answer is, "VERY good!" These beautifully illustrated cards will help you get there.

ACKNOWLEDGMENTS

Working on this book was balm for my soul. I'll begin my thanks with Alice herself. I'm grateful for her playfulness, kindness, and the way she doesn't take my neurotic tendencies, out of control fears, and wild bouts of self-pity too seriously. I'm grateful for her graciousness and I look forward to future collaborations.

I'm thankful for all the friends on Instagram and Facebook who have cheered Alice and me on:

Paula Williams, Maria Woods, Lisa Yahne, Robin Mooney, Suzi Vandersteen, April Harries, Jessica Rossing, Victoria Loustalot, Laura Braafladt, Gia Duke, Mary Kay Beraducci, Emily Christenson, Barbara Swift, Sara Taylor, Kristy Marie, Jen LeGrand Reiter, and Amanda Imes.

This book would not exist without the kindly and gentle editing and guidance provided by the one and only Grace Kerina.

A profound bow to CharLee of Wonder Loft Creative for her elegant design and unprecedented creative work on both the book and card deck! You are an amazing momma, human and designer! Thank you.

Finally, thanks to Mark for always believing in me.

ALSO BY
SARAH BAMFORD SEIDELMANN

The Book of Beasties: Your A to Z Guide to the Illuminating Wisdom of Spirit Animals

The Book of Beasties invites you to explore why certain animals show up in your life and what teachings they may be trying to share. Packed with information, illustrations, and traditional and modern insights into the unique qualities of different beasties.

> *"Just got my copy of* The Book of Beasties. *I love* Animal Speak, *by Ted Andrews... and now there's a new kid on the block—Sarah Seidelmann! This book is incredible. It is SO GOOD!!"*
>
> **—Christiane Northrup, MD**

Born to FREAK: A Salty Primer for Irrepressible Humans

I believe we were all born to FREAK. We were all put here not to fit in, but to see things differently, to ruffle feathers, and to return balance to the world and our communities by using our creative abilities, our healing presence, and our eccentric gifts. I wrote this book to help you discover your own wondrous inner multitudes, so you'll share your fantastic, strange, and entirely original notions with the world. We need you.

Swimming with Elephants: My Unexpected Pilgrimage from Physician to Healer

Swimming with Elephants tells the eccentric, sometimes poignant, and occasionally hilarious experience of a working mother undergoing a bewildering vocational shift from physician to shamanic healer. During that tumultuous period of answering her call, Sarah met an elephant (Alice!) who would become an important spirit companion on her journey, had bones thrown for her by a shaman in South Africa, and traveled to India for an ancient Hindu pilgrimage, where she received the blessing she had been longing for. Ultimately, she discovered an entirely different way of healing, one that she had always aspired to, and that enabled her to help those who are suffering.

> *"A fascinating, amusing, and wise account of how someone born with a shaman's predilections, raised in a rationalist culture, finds her way back to her true self."*
>
> **—Martha Beck, New York Times bestselling author of *Expecting Adam***

What the Walrus Knows
app for
iPad and iPhone

Follow Your
FEEL GOOD

HOW GOOD ARE YOU WILLING TO LET IT GET?

Made in the USA
Monee, IL
12 August 2021